Trauma
Narrative responses to Traumatic experience

Edited by David Denborough

The papers in this book were originally published in the
International Journal of Narrative Therapy and Community Work

DULWICH CENTRE PUBLICATIONS
Adelaide, South Australia

ISBN 0 9752180 3 4

Proof Reading:
Jane Hales

Contents

Introduction

by David Denborough

In recent years, the field of 'trauma work' has grown exponentially. This increased interest in these matters seems to offer many possibilities as well as a range of hazards! There is so much to consider. Putting together this book has meant witnessing more than usual the violence, trauma and abuse, that is a part of life for many people. It has also meant coming to know about inspiring work in different parts of the world by individuals and organisations dedicated to responding to trauma in ways that make a difference. Stories of work from Bangladesh, Sri Lanka, Palestine, Israel, South Africa and Australia are included in these pages. We hope that these stories will spark conversations in your own context and lead to continuing creativity in your own work.

Some of the questions that are considered in this book include:

- Chapter One: How can workers understand their experiences in this area? Notions of 'vicarious trauma' are now commonplace and it is regularly assumed that therapists and counsellors can become traumatised themselves by witnessing stories of trauma. Are there alternative ways of understanding and responding to workers' experience?

- Chapter Two: How can narrative ideas inform work with people who are suffering the consequences of multiple trauma?

- Chapter Three: Understandings about trauma and trauma work that have been developed in western countries are now being 'exported' across cultures. What are the implications of this, and how can care be taken not to replicate forms of psychological colonisation?

- Chapter Four: The concept of trauma de-briefing has been the focus of considerable debate in recent years. Are there ways in which narrative ideas can be helpful when meeting with people who have recently experienced trauma?

- Chapter Five: When receiving and documenting the testimonies of those who have been subjected to trauma, violence and abuse, how can this be done in ways that are not re-traumatising and that, instead, contribute to redressing the effects of trauma in a person's life? How can these testimonies then be used for broader purposes?

- Chapter Six: When therapists, or their loved ones, experience significant trauma themselves, how does this influence their work?

- Chapter Seven: When working with children who have endured significant trauma, how can we ensure our conversations do not contribute to re-traumatisation? How can we provide an alternative territory of identity for these children to stand in as they begin to give voice to their experiences?

- Chapter Eight: When one's work is occurring in a context of occupation, and the trauma that people are experiencing is not past or post, but is continuing, how can workers respond?

- Chapter Nine: When working in a context like the Acid Survivors Foundation in Bangladesh, how can narrative ideas assist to unearth and thicken the values that shape our work?

- Chapter Ten: What are some of the considerations when working with a heterosexual couple in which both partners have experienced trauma?

- Chapter Eleven: What principles and practices can contribute to a 'Healing of memories' in countries and communities that have experienced widespread trauma and violence?

    As I mentioned above, there is so much to consider!

    I hope this book will support you in your work.

CHAPTER ONE

How can you do this work?

Responding to questions about the experience of working with women who were subjected to child sexual abuse

by Sue Mann

This chapter explores ways of understanding the experience of therapists who work in the field of child sexual abuse. The author describes how she is regularly asked by women who consult her, 'How can you do this work?' The first section of this chapter explores the different meanings that this question can have for those women who ask it of their therapist. The second section considers the many different experiences that the author has in counseling conversations with women who have been subjected to child sexual abuse. The final section particularly focuses on those experiences of therapist distress that sometimes accompany this sort of work. A range of questions are provided in the hope that these will be helpful to other therapists.

Introduction

When I was first asked the question 'How can you do this work?' by a woman who was meeting with me around the effects of child sexual abuse in her life, her question took me by surprise. It was asked in a way that suggested that it must be either 'hard', in an onerous way, or 'depressing' or 'upsetting' for me to be hearing about her experiences of sexual abuse. I had a sense that it implied that my experience of our counselling sessions couldn't be anything other than difficult. Since that time, other women have asked me the same question. Sometimes women have let me know that they are aware I am meeting with many women around these issues. They have expressed a curiosity about what it means for me to be hearing all day from women about their experience of abuse and its effects in their life.

Initially, I was surprised to realise that women meeting with me could imagine that my primary experience of this work would involve difficulty, depression and/or upset.

This realisation raised further questions for me. I wondered if the women were thinking that somehow I might have to be hardened to this listening, or extraordinarily clever, or professionally detached if I was not to be affected in negative ways by hearing from them. I wondered if they imagined that finding ways not to be affected by this work was a part of doing it. These reflections have encouraged me to consider the complexities in responding to the question of 'How can you do this work?' This paper is an exploration of some of these complexities.

In this paper I am interested in exploring two questions:

- Firstly, how can I respond to women when they ask me: 'How can you do this work?'

- And secondly, how can we as counsellors explore the meaning of our experiences of this work?

PART ONE:
Responding to women when they ask this question

In order to consider ways of responding to the question: 'How can you do this work?' it first seems important to explore what this question might mean for the women who ask it of us.

I would like to begin by describing the contribution that a woman called Cathy has made to my thinking about these issues. Cathy consulted me about the effects of abuse in her childhood. When we first met, Cathy told me that she knew that she needed to tell someone about the abuse she had experienced, but she felt so concerned for me as a counsellor to hear these things that she was reluctant to begin. I heard from Cathy that she had not been able to speak to other counsellors about her experiences in the past partly because of this concern. I asked Cathy were there any questions that she might like to ask me that would support her to begin to speak about the abuse. These were her questions to me:

- What experience have you had in counselling around abuse?

- What is it like for you to hear about abuse?

- What supports do you have in the workplace?

- What are your ideas about counselling and how it works with people like me?

In responding to these questions, I also let Cathy know that I was curious about what these questions of hers might reflect about her preferences in life, and what she knew about what might suit her in telling of her experiences about the effects of abuse. Some of the questions I asked Cathy included:

- Do you have some ideas about the kind of telling that would be helpful to you?

- Have you experienced telling in the past that has been helpful?

- What do you think makes up a helpful or not so helpful telling for you?

- What kind of listening assists in the kind of telling that you would like to have?

Cathy was quick to let me know that the kind of telling that was important to her was the kind that would mean that the abuse stopped here, that her telling would not be about abuse continuing to have a destructive, harmful, negative or traumatic influence in the lives of others. This included my life as her counsellor. We then considered other questions including:

- Throughout our meetings, how can we continue to know if this telling is helpful or not?

- Are there other people who might support you in the telling of these hard things?

This conversation with Cathy has stayed with me as a reminder of what it can mean for women to take the first steps in speaking out about aspects of their lives that have been so powerfully silenced. It also reminds me of the commitments that accompany women's wish to speak out and that inform their preferences for how this sharing can take place.

Within counselling sessions, concerns such as Cathy's are quite common. I regularly hear from women about worries they have in relation to what it will be like for me to hear about the abuse they experienced. This concern is often expressed to me through questions like: 'How can you do this work?', 'Doesn't this affect you too?', 'How do you look after yourself?', and so on. It is also sometimes expressed in other ways. For example, many women prepare me, in thoughtful ways, to hear what they want to speak about. Some women have let me know in advance that there are some very hard things that they want to talk about in relation to the abuse and they want to know if it will be okay for me to hear about these things. Sometimes women have also asked how I am supported in the work and occasionally I have been asked directly what it is like for me to hear about abuse from so many different women.

I would like to consider four themes in responding to the question: 'How can you do this work'.

1. The first involves trying to understand how women's concerns might relate to their past experiences of trying to talk about the abuse and the history of silencing and disbelief that they may have experienced.

2. The second involves considerations about how therapy works.

3. The third involves understanding about how abuse can affect people's lives and their experiences of themselves.

4. And fourthly, as mentioned above in my conversations with Cathy, what the intentions, values and commitments may be that are influencing why a woman may care about my experience of listening to her.

   I will now briefly consider each of these themes.

Past experiences of talking about abuse

Often I hear from women who are meeting with me for counselling around the effects of abuse that they have had previous experiences of feeling responsible for causing distress to other counsellors or friends and family members. These women have a heightened sense of the possible negative effects of speaking about abuse. Some women have shared with me how others have responded to them in the past. For instance, they may have been told: 'This is too hard for me', or 'I can't listen to what you are talking about'. Some women have told me that others have become so upset in hearing about abuse from them that they have been unable to talk further about it. Hearing about these experiences from the women has led me to reflect on my own work and how the women might experience my responses to their stories of abuse. This has led me to be very interested in the meanings the women have taken from those experiences. When women ask me the question: 'How can you do this work?', I am interested in hearing about how their past experiences of talking about the abuse may have contributed to some of the concerns they bring to our conversations.

Frequently, women bring to these conversations a long history of being silenced in relation to the abuse – not only by the person who abused them, but by other significant adults in their lives who have not believed them, and by a more general societal discourse that tends to disbelieve women's stories of abuse (Linnell & Cora 1993).

Recognising that so many women have had these experiences in beginning to talk about abuse shapes what I hear when a woman asks me: 'How can you do this work?'

Understandings about therapy

In trying to understand the significance for women of asking about my experience of being a counsellor, I have come to realise that there are particular assumptions about counselling that contribute to women's concerns. Many of the women who have consulted me have told me that their concern for me relates to the idea that counselling is a place where someone comes to 'let it all out' or 'get it all out'. This idea that someone comes to therapy to 'dump' the abuse in the therapeutic space seems pervasive. It is an idea that the women have often picked up from personal experiences of counselling, or from hearing from other people about their experiences of counselling, or through books, and films. I have even had one woman apologise to me for 'dumping all that ... on you'.

In considering the many effects of this understanding of therapy, I have at times responded by describing that what is important to me in listening to them will be what Michael White refers to as 'double-listening' (2004). I try to let women know that, not only do I want to listen to the effects that the abuse has had in their lives, but also to some of the other stories of people's lives that have been silenced, unspoken, unacknowledged or relegated to the sidelines. I am interested in letting the women know that I will be listening not only to the negative stories but also to stories about their beliefs and values and hopes and dreams. I want to be clear that abuse is not the only story to be told and that I will be listening for alternative stories. These may be stories of resistance – their refusal to kiss their grandfather goodbye may no longer be seen as an example of 'a naughty girl' but instead an attempt to resist the abuse. They may also be stories of care, protection of others, stories about loving or tolerance, stories of courage or inventiveness or imagination.

The effects of abuse

When women first speak with me they frequently describe themselves to me in ways that are about 'worthlessness', 'self-doubt' and 'self-loathing'. They sometimes use phrases such as being 'damaged goods' or 'broken' or even 'hateful'. In hearing these descriptions, I am aware that I am hearing the 'voice of abuse'. I am hearing women's descriptions of themselves as if through the eyes of the abuse. When a woman then asks me: 'How can you do this work?', I try to think about what influence the voice of abuse may be playing in our conversations now.

Women have told me that when they first spoke to me about the effects of abuse they were worried that I was going to confirm to them that they were 'crazy', or 'mad', or in some way responsible for the abuse. They spoke to me about the abuse despite a strong sense that there was every chance that I would think that they asked for the abuse by being 'promiscuous' as a child, or that they were 'naughty' or 'weak' because they didn't tell anyone earlier, or that I would think that they wanted the abuse because they didn't stop it, or that I would minimise its effects because it wasn't 'violent' or because the person who was abusive was also kind at times.

When I hear the question: 'How can you do this work?', it draws my attention to what the women may have had to overcome to speak to me about the effects of abuse in their lives. It draws my attention to how the interpretations of others may still be playing a significant part in how the woman may understand herself. She may be under the influence of stories about her life that attempt to convince her that she is worthless or to blame. And these influences may also contribute to her thinking that my experience of speaking to her will necessarily be negative.

This realisation is also a source of hopefulness for me in the work. Because, despite the effects of abuse, this person has chosen to speak of her experiences and to begin to question some of the ways of seeing herself that may have adopted a truth status in her life. At these times, Michael White's idea of the 'absent but implicit' is significant to me (2000). The idea that expressions of pain may represent a testimony to certain values that have been transgressed or violated, opens up directions for us to explore together. The person I am meeting with is therefore not someone who I think of as being 'damaged' by abuse, but instead is someone with values, hopes, dreams and commitments that have been violated by the abuse. It provides an opportunity for us to explore what those values may be, their history and why they are precious.

Values and intentions in asking the question

This leads us back to the conversation with Cathy that I mentioned initially. When a woman asks me: 'How can you do this work?', I am very interested to enquire about the values that inform her question. In Cathy's instance, she was very clear that the abuse stopped here. She was committed to ensuring that the experiences she was subjected to did not continue to have a destructive, harmful, negative or traumatic influence in the lives of others, including in my life. This was very important to Cathy in how our conversations proceeded, and I came to hear how this was a strongly held value in her life.

In hearing about important values that people hold, it is possible to ask more questions about them. It becomes possible to ask questions about the history of these commitments around care and concern. It becomes possible to hear stories about how these commitments have featured in other valued relationships in the woman's life. It becomes possible to learn about territories of life that have been protected from the effects of abuse.

There are a number of things that I want to consider and keep close to mind when someone asks the question: 'How can you do this work?'. These are considerations about the influence of histories of silencing; about the effects of certain understandings of therapy; about the effects of abuse; and also the values and commitments that may be informing the question. I am interested in not making assumptions about what this question might mean to the woman concerned.

Finding ways of responding to the question: 'How do you do this work?' that honour women's intentions in asking the question, and that don't in any way contribute to further silencing of them, has been challenging to me.

At this stage, there are a range of different responses that I might give depending upon the context:

- Sometimes, I may ask more about what the particular woman might need to know about my experience of the work that would assist her to talk about what is important to her. She may then ask other questions such as: 'Do you take the stories home with you?', 'Who else do you talk to about this?' These questions provide opportunities for me to talk about the ways that I experience support in my work. They also provide a chance to be transparent about organisational practices of supervision, confidentiality, documentation, and other workplace practices in ways that assist women to make informed decisions about what they will talk to me about.

- Sometimes it seems important to acknowledge that there are times when I do feel sad or distressed in relation to hearing about stories of abuse. I do not remain neutral in hearing about abuse and I try to articulate why this is important to me.

- Sometimes I speak about the wide range of responses that I have to this work – responses that range from sorrow, puzzlement, delight and connection.

- Sometimes I describe how much I learn from each conversation and how my consultations with one woman assist in working with others. I let them know that the conversations I am sharing with this particular woman will assist me in talking with others.

- Sometimes I describe that when I listen to women I am not only on the lookout for the ways that abuse has influenced their lives, but also for the other stories of women's lives that have been treasured and nurtured over the years but have had little opportunity to be shared with others. I mention that I am always interested in hearing about relationships that may have supported women over years.

- Frequently, I acknowledge the contributions that other women who have spoken to me in the past about their experiences of abuse make to my work. I want to let the woman know how much I draw on the knowledge of these other women, and that I couldn't be doing this work in the same way without the support of these past conversations.

- I am interested in learning more about why the question is important to the women, what values and commitments it may be related to. And, if relevant, I then want to find ways to have these richly described.

- Finally, I am interested in checking back with the women about the effects of my responses; whether what I have said is of interest to the woman concerned, and whether there are any other questions that may be good to talk about (Morgan 2000).

PART TWO:

What does the question: *'How can you do this work?' mean to me?*

As I reflect on the question: 'How can you do this work?', I am aware that my experience of counselling varies on different days, during the course of one day, and even within one conversation! I am also aware that I am sometimes asked this question outside the context of therapy – by friends, family members, or new acquaintances. Whenever it is asked it makes me think about the multiplicity of experiences of hearing from women about the gross betrayals of trust, the trickery, the pain and hurt of child sexual abuse.

In the course of a week, I might have the following experiences within counselling conversations:

- *Outrage* as I hear from someone about the subtle and deliberate ways the sports coach gained the trust of adults in the family and then went on to sexually abuse all the children in the family.

- Shared *excitement* with a woman who has embraced an understanding that she is not to blame for the abuse that was perpetrated on her.

- *Inspiration* in relation to the commitments a young woman shares with me around a particular stand she has taken in her life to protect other children from the person who abused her, even though this may put her own safety at risk.

- A *sense of pleasure* in noticing with women the ways that many of the people in their lives contribute to life in ethical and caring ways.

- *Distress* in relation to how insidiously the words of the person who has abused still influence and have a say in a woman's life fifty years after these words were spoken.

- *Laughter* and *joy* in relation to the boldness and humour of some of the strategies women have developed to reclaim their lives from the effects of abuse.

- *Concern, worry* and *fear* for the safety of particular women either in relation to possible acts of self-harm, or in relation to violence from which they are at risk.

- *Hopefulness* about what speaking about the abuse might offer the women in having less of these effects of abuse in their lives.

- *Despair* at how some people in positions of power and influence use that power to abuse the vulnerable.

- Deep *sadness* in coming to understand what it meant to small children to have to somehow make sense of the abuse in total isolation.

- *Shared pleasure* as a woman puts a name to another story of her life that reflects her commitments to care for herself and others, and that can be traced back to acts she took to protect herself and her siblings during their childhood. Such a story might be named 'the great escape' or 'a life dedicated to protecting and caring for children'.

There are, of course, many other aspects of the work that I could describe here, but I hope this list gives some sense of the multiple meanings that my counselling work has for me.

What I would like to do now is consider in more detail what it is that makes this work sustainable. To me, that is what the question: 'How do you do this work?' is really asking. What makes my work sustainable includes taking care with how I listen and respond to stories of trauma and abuse and how I am supported in doing so, and also finding ways to acknowledge and celebrate with others the positive stories of this work.

Isolation and community

One of the first things I noticed in working with women who experienced child sexual abuse was the powerful effect of isolation in their lives. I heard from women how the person who perpetrated the abuse had deliberately isolated them as children. This isolation occurred through threats, manipulations and by confusing the children. The isolation took a range of forms:

- It involved isolation from other supportive adults who might have protected them as a child.

- It involved isolation from other children who were also being abused by the same person. If these children had been able to speak to each other about their experiences this could have contributed to different meanings being made about the abuse.

- Over time, the women had been separated and isolated from any knowledge of their responses to what was being done to them (White 2004).

- They had also often been disconnected and isolated from what was important to them – their key values, hopes and commitments (White 2004).

Many women have spoken to me about the effects of these forms of isolation and what they have meant in their life. For children to be isolated in their attempts to make sense of events of abuse creates a context for feelings of shame, doubt, guilt, anxiety and fear to flourish.

When one aspect of therapeutic practice with women who have experienced child sexual abuse involves noticing the effects of this isolation, it seems ironic that therapists can often work in contexts of isolation themselves. Therapeutic conversations often occur between two individuals. Therapists are often physically separated from each other in the workplace. And some organisational practices, such as individual supervision, tend to support an individualised approach to therapeutic work.

In saying this, I don't mean to disregard that some women have a clear preference for seeking individual consultations. Nor do I want to downplay the ways in which therapists may engage with re-membering conversations and outsider-witness practices in their work with individuals (Mann & Russell 2002). And, of course, many organisations bring women together in therapeutic groups, ongoing support groups, shared counselling experiences, educational forums, and/or family therapy programs and/or provide peer support for workers.

However, I also want to consider how some workplace processes may inadvertently perpetuate isolating practices. I have become particularly interested in being on the lookout for:

- workplace practices that might contribute to therapists/counsellors being left on their own to make sense of challenging and complex work experiences;

- practices that might contribute to separation and divisions between colleagues. These include comparative or competitive practices that imply that workers are required to 'measure up' to a particular definition of what makes a successful worker;

- assumptions that might prevent workers from speaking about some of the dilemmas in the work. These include the assumption that workers individually ought to 'have all the answers';

- practices that might separate therapists/counsellors from their own knowledge of what they bring to therapeutic conversations in terms of ideas, experiences and particular commitments, values, and so on.

For each of these workplace practices that leave room for isolation there are alternative practices that support connection in this work. For instance:

- practices that create forums where it is possible for workers to speak about challenging and complex experiences of the work;

- practices that enable workers to speak about and contribute to discussions around the many different ways that the work can be done;

- basing a workplace culture on the idea that, rather than individuals having to 'possess' the answers, answers can instead be generated through conversation and collaboration;

- developing workplace conversations and processes that acknowledge the unique ideas, experiences and commitments of each worker.

It has been through hearing from women about the effects of isolation in their lives that I have come to appreciate that I am not exempt from the influence of prevailing cultural isolating practices that work to separate people from one another. In considering this, I have become more aware that what makes my work sustainable are practices of collaboration. Sharing a commitment with others to notice practices that might work to isolate or separate us in the workplace strongly supports me. It supports me not only in finding ways to resist isolating practices but also in considering creative ways to keep conversation and collaboration more present in my work.

I have come to appreciate even more that what is important to me in standing against isolation is the notion of community. I want to think about my work not as a singular endeavour but as part of collaborative and community attempts to address issues of abuse and violence. This notion of community also influences the attention I pay to asking questions about the relationships that sustain the women I am talking with. These might have been relationships during their childhood, or current connections with friends, children, partners or support groups. They may even be relationships with those who are no longer alive.

This orientation to community also influences my own sense of the work. In writing these words, I am reminded of the community of people who I carry with me in my counselling work. This community is made up of the people who have consulted me in the past, my work mates, colleagues, friends, family, and authors who have shared their thinking via the written word. This is a community of people with whom I share particular commitments to challenge the social and cultural practices that contribute to abuses of power. This is a community that I value. In keeping connected to this community, I know that I am not alone in the work. I am also constantly reminded that any attempts to respond to abuse and violence are not singular efforts, they are linked to shared knowledge, commitments, and actions that many people are taking in a vast array of contexts.

PART THREE:
Understanding and responding to distress/sorrow in this work

Recently, I have noticed that increasing attention is being paid to the effects on counsellors, crisis workers, police, ambulance workers, etc, who listen to, or witness traumatic and/or abusive events in people's lives (Weingarten 2003). In the counselling field, this interest has particularly focused on workers' experiences of distress, sadness or fatigue; ways of understanding these experiences; and methods of support for workers (Richardson 2001).

This recent attention has encouraged me to think further about ways of understanding the 'hard parts' of this work. It has invited me to consider ideas of wellbeing and self-care in relation to hearing from women about the abuse they have experienced. It has also had me thinking about how we understand possible experiences of distress, sorrow, shock and upset that can at times accompany this work.

Before I discuss the various ways I might consider responding to these experiences of distress and sadness, I first want to acknowledge that I am working in a supportive environment, in a well-resourced organisation, in safe circumstances. The chances of me experiencing violence in my daily life are very slim. This is not true for all counsellors. I do not want to assume that what is relevant to me in my context is relevant to those who are working in very different circumstances.

In this section, I will offer some understandings that I find helpful to think about when I notice feelings of distress, burden, sorrow, or a sense of being overwhelmed in relation to my counselling work with women survivors of childhood sexual abuse. I offer them here in the hope that they may be helpful to other therapists and that this can contribute to further conversations on this topic.

Ways of understanding experiences of therapist distress
An opportunity to acknowledge what is being noticed

Distress does not occur by chance. In my experience, it often reflects some new learning, or realisation that has occurred through hearing particular stories about abuse and trauma. Therefore, feelings of distress can provide an opportunity to put a name to and to reflect upon what it is that a therapist may be noticing differently. This could include a new awareness about certain understandings about life. For example, the therapist may have realised that they have gained a greater knowledge about the extent of abuse in the world, or lost an unawareness in relation to the extent of abuse and hardship in the world. Or, a therapist's distress may relate to new realisations about the experience of those who have been subjected to abuse (for instance the extent of the fear that may have accompanied someone's early life, or the practices of power and entrapment that they were subjected to). Alternatively, feelings of distress may relate to the ways in which a particular story has confirmed the therapist's own experiences of life (for example, a particular story may powerfully resonate with aspects of a therapist's personal experience).

These feelings of distress can be opportunities to develop, revise and think more about our ideas about the world and about the sorts of lives we wish to lead. They are an opportunity to consider how this can be taken into conversations with others.

An opportunity to acknowledge values, wishes and hopes

A counsellor's distress might say something about what is important to the counsellor. It might indicate that certain values, wishes and hopes that s/he has about the world have been transgressed in some way (White 2000, 2004). I am interested in understanding the meaning of this distress for a counsellor. It might have occurred in relation to hearing particular stories, or witnessing or participating in certain workplace practices. This distress can be an opportunity to hear more from the counsellor about the important values, hopes, dreams and wishes that they have for how the world should be and about the history of these values. Experiencing distress can therefore be an opportunity to have these values, wishes and hopes spoken about and more richly storied. This, in turn, can provide a foundation for further action that is in accordance with these values and wishes. Creating opportunities to understand the distress they may experience as related to certain cherished values they hold provides different avenues for conversation, support and action. This has become an important understanding for me in my work. If I am feeling particularly moved or upset by a certain conversation, I am now also interested in thinking through, and talking with others:

- Why was this conversation or series of conversations particularly significant to me?

- Does my upset or distress relate to certain beliefs, values, wishes, hopes that are important to me?

- Why are these values significant to me?

- How can I find connection with others around these values in my work and the rest of my life?

- What further action might I be able to take in relation to my work that would fit with these values?

An opportunity to consider workplace practices

One of the understandings that assists me if I notice that I am struggling in the work, is to consider whether certain stories of my work are being neglected. I am interested in exploring other themes that may have been neglected or overlooked and need to be brought forward. I am particularly interested in ways that this can be done that stand against isolation; I want to consider how conversations about these other neglected stories can be shared and witnessed. A therapist's distress may therefore be an opportunity to consider generating organisational practices to enable workers to richly describe the commitments, beliefs, hopes and values that influence each person's work. It might be an opportunity to consider how there can be a more collective sharing of stories of the work. Questions worth considering might include:

- What opportunities are available for workers to talk about the many experiences of the work?

- Of the many different stories of work that could be shared, what stories and whose stories are being privileged?

- How are the connections people have to what is important and of value to them shared in the workplace?

- What opportunities are there for celebrations in relation to the achievements in the work?

- Are there opportunities to share moments of sadness, moments of beauty, moments of joy?

An opportunity to reconnect with local knowledge and relationships

Some understandings about therapy locate the therapist's knowledge and interventions at the centre of change. This understanding can contribute to experiences of despair and burnout. A therapist's fatigue, or sense of burden, can become an opportunity to reconnect with the significance of local knowledge, skills and histories of experience in addressing the effects of trauma and abuse. Rather than thinking that we as therapists can independently assist people to deal with the effects of child sexual abuse, notions of de-centred practice enable us to consider how we bring into our conversations the skills and knowledge of those who are consulting us. Questions to consider might include:

- How is the work valuing and building on the contributions of the community of people that might support those we are meeting with?

- Are we finding ways to document, and create an audience for, the skills and knowledge that the women with whom we meet have demonstrated in responding to the effects of abuse in their lives?

There are many people who find ways to reclaim their lives from the effects of trauma without ever consulting professional help. Keeping an awareness of this assists me to privilege the many aspects of local knowledge and relationships that support people in dealing with these effects. This can include: the care from significant others who have never given up on the person concerned, or whose image and faith in the person has never waned; acts of self-care that have offered sustenance; the role of spirituality; political movements; pets; connection to the earth, rivers, oceans, and so on. I am interested in how we can ensure that the role of the therapist is not valorised over the everyday acts of meaning-making that support people in surviving trauma and abuse. I am interested in how local knowledge can be valued, especially when we are trying to understand therapists' experience of their work.

An opportunity to connect with others around the politics of the work

An individual therapist's distress is also an opportunity to notice, name and connect with others around the politics of the work. Responses to violence against women originated within a collective, political feminist movement and as therapeutic practice has become the primary way in which violence against women is now responded to, various writers have raised concerns about how this individualises and depoliticises the issue. Whenever an individual therapist is distressed at the stories being heard, this can also be an opportunity for re-connecting with wider feminist consciousness and political action. Distress can be an opportunity to not leave these issues in the private, individual realm. Questions to consider might include:

- Who else would be most likely to share this sense of distress/outrage?

- How could we come together to take some form of action as an outcome of this distress?

- How can the ideas and understandings gained in the conversations of therapy inform organisational responses, policy, legislative responses, education of other therapists?

- How can what is talked about in the therapeutic conversations connect women with each other around their common experience of life in ways that enable broader social action?

- How are the politics of gender, class, race, age and heterosexual dominance being named and responded to within the conversations that are occurring in therapy and by the organisation more broadly?

An opportunity to acknowledge that what is sometimes most distressing is not the stories we are hearing

Sometimes what is most distressing in a workplace is not so much to do with the stories being shared in counselling conversations but more to do with other aspects of the work. For example, when I was working as a hospital social worker, one of the most difficult challenges for me and colleagues in our department were the ways in which women were spoken of and treated by those in positions of authority. At different times I experienced this as distressing. Some of my colleagues and I tried different ways of responding to this situation. These included: asking questions about people's intentions in speaking this way; raising the matter in formal ways at organisational meetings; and trying to demonstrate an alternative way of relating within the wards. I often had a sense that nothing changed in spite of this and was at times feeling considerable despair about this.

A response that made a key difference to me was offered by a therapist who worked in a different setting[1]. After a discussion together about the political nature of this work and the efforts that we were making to try to influence the hospital culture, this colleague gave me a small plastic figurine of a deep sea diver. She described that she thought this image of a deep sea diver related to the work we were engaged with. The actions we were taking were frequently quiet, un-noticed and underground (or underwater in the case of the diver!). And yet they were also productive, hard-working, busy and seeing the world from a different perspective. I stuck this deep sea diver figurine to the front of my diary and it accompanied me to ward rounds, allocation meetings, case conferences, and planning meetings. It provided a visual reminder to me of the important preferences that I had for my work as well as a tangible reminder of my connection to others who shared these values and understandings. It wasn't so much the nature of the conversations I was sharing with hospital patients that was causing me distress but more the actions of disrespect within the hospital culture. This has stayed with me as a reminder that experiences of sadness or distress in my work as a therapist might not be due to the stories I am hearing. Questions that may be relevant to consider include:

- Does the distress relate to the stories that are being heard in the counselling sessions or to other interactions in the workplace or home life?

- If other areas are the source of the distress, are there ways of seeking support in relation to this?

An opportunity to consider the real effects of different understandings of a therapist's distress

The ways in which we understand therapist distress or sadness will have differing effects on our work, our lives, and on the lives of those who consult us. Whenever we are engaged in conversations about experiences of our work, how can we keep this in mind? A question that might be relevant to include is:

- How can we take care so that the ways in which we understand our experience of therapeutic work honour the multiple contributions that women who consult with us make to our lives and work?

An opportunity to link with others

Whenever I experience distress or sadness in relation to my counselling work with women, I am now determined to ensure that I am not isolated in this experience. Each of the themes listed above has become a source of conversation with friends, family members, colleagues, or within formal supervision.

I would be very interested to hear from you about whether these sorts of explorations about your experiences of your work are helpful.

Reflection

The question: 'How can you do this work?' was first asked of me several years ago and I have been thinking about it ever since! The conversations I have had with other women, colleagues and friends have influenced the ways that I think about what sustains me and how I might respond when I experience distress related to this work.

In the first section of this paper, I tried to explore the varied meanings that the question: 'How can you do this work?' can have for those women who ask it of their therapist.

In the second section, I tried to describe what this question means to me and how it invites me to consider the many different experiences that I have in counselling conversations with women who have been subjected to child sexual abuse.

In the final section, I tried to particularly focus on those experiences of distress that sometimes accompany this sort of work. I have tried to provide a range of questions that I now find helpful to think through whenever I may feel overwhelmed.

I hope that these reflections and questions will contribute to your own conversations around what makes this work sustainable for you, and your own responses to the question: 'How can we do this work?'

Acknowledgements

Thinking about my experience of counselling is a continuing project. What I have been able to write about here is an outcome of the many conversations with women such as Cathy who have consulted with me and who have been a part of this journey of learning with me. It is also an outcome of many conversations with colleagues. I'd like to especially acknowledge my colleagues that I worked with at Uniting Care Wesley, and within my current supportive workplace, RespondSA. I would particularly like to acknowledge the ongoing contribution to my work of Andrew Groome who has been a colleague in this work for several years. Conversations with those at Women's Health Statewide and at Dulwich Centre have also been very significant to me. In particular, I would like to thank David Denborough for his encouragement, editorial direction and understandings with this writing. The comments on an earlier draft by Jodie Sloan and Alice Morgan were very helpful.

Note

1. This therapist was Leela Anderson from whom I was receiving supervision at the time.

References / Resources

Birchmore. K. 2003: 'Not the Only One'. *Spring Newsletter of Women's Health Statewide*. Adelaide: Women's Health Statewide.

Cora, D. & Linnell, S. 1993: *Discoveries: A Group Resource for Women Who Have Been Sexually Abused in Childhood*. Sydney, NSW: Dympna House.

Gavey, N. 1999: '"I Wasn't Raped, but ..."' Revisiting definitional problems in sexual victimization.' In Lamb, S. (ed): *New Versions of Victims: Feminists struggle with the concept*. New York: New York University Press.

Haaken, J. 1999: 'Heretical Texts: The courage to heal and the incest survivor movement'. In Lamb, S. (ed) *New Versions of Victims: Feminists struggle with the concept*. New York: New York University Press.

Hermann, J 1992: *Trauma and Recovery: The aftermath of violence – from domestic violence to political terror*. New York: Basic Books.

Kitzinger, C. & Perkins, R. 1993: *Changing Our Minds: Lesbian feminism and psychology*. New York: New York University Press.

Lamb, S. 1999: 'Constructing the victim: Popular images and lasting labels'. In Lamb, S. (ed): *New Versions of Victims: Feminists Struggle with the Concept*. New York: New York University Press.

Mann, S. & Russell, S. 2002: 'Narrative ways of working with women survivors of childhood sexual abuse.' *International Journal of Narrative Therapy and Community Work*, 3:3-22. Republished 2003 in Dulwich Centre Publications (eds): *Responding to Violence: A collection of papers relating to child sexual abuse and violence in intimate relationships*, pp. 1-34 (chapter 1). Adelaide: Dulwich Centre Publications.

McPhie, L. & Chaffey, C. 1998: 'The journey of a lifetime: Group work with young women who have experienced sexual assault.' *Gecko: a journal of deconstruction and narrative ideas in therapeutic practice*, 1:3-34. Republished 1999 in Dulwich Centre Publications (eds): *Extending Narrative Therapy: A collection of practice-based papers* (chapter 4), pp. 31-61. Adelaide: Dulwich Centre Publications.

Morgan, A. 2000: *What is Narrative Therapy? An easy-to-read introduction*. Adelaide: Dulwich Centre Publications.

Morris, A. 2003: *Working with Maternal Alienation in Domestic/Family Violence and Child Sexual Abuse*. Adelaide: Northern Metro Community Health Service, Women's Health Statewide & University of Adelaide.

Myerhoff, B. 1982: 'Life history among the elderly: Performance, visibility and remembering.' In Ruby, J. (ed): *A Crack in the Mirror: Reflexive Perspectives in Anthropology*. Philadelphia: University of Pennsylvania Press.

Neame, A. & Heenan, M. 2003: 'What lies behind the hidden figure of sexual assault: Issues of prevalence and disclosure'. *Briefing #1* September 2003 Melbourne: Australian Institute of Family Studies.

O'Leary, P. 1998: 'Liberation from self-blame: Working with men who have experienced childhood sexual abuse.' *Dulwich Centre Journal*, 4:24-40. Republished 1999 in Dulwich Centre Publications (eds): *Extending Narrative Therapy: A collection of practice-based papers* (chapter 12), pp. 159-187.

Richardson, J. 2001: *Guidebook on Vicarious Trauma: Recommended solutions for anti-violence workers*. Ontario, Canada: National Clearinghouse on Family Violence.

Russell, S. 2005: 'Examining discourse when talking with women.' *International Journal of Narrative Therapy and Community Work*, 1:53-57.

Silent Too Long, 1998: 'Your voices inspire mine.' *Dulwich Centre Journal*, 4:2-8.

Silent Too Long, 2000: 'Embracing the old, nurturing the new.' *Dulwich Centre Journal*, 1&2:62-71. Republished 2003 in Dulwich Centre Publications (eds): *Responding to Violence: A collection of papers relating to child sexual abuse and violence in intimate relationships*, pp. 71-91 (chapter 3). Adelaide: Dulwich Centre Publications.

Taylor, C. 2004: *Surviving the Legal System: A handbook for adult and child sexual assault survivors and their supporters*. Melbourne: Coulomb Communications.

Verco, J. 2002: 'Women's outrage and the pressure to forgive.' *International Journal of Narrative Therapy and Community Work*, 1:23-27. Republished 2003 in Dulwich Centre Publications (eds): *Responding to Violence: A collection of papers relating to child sexual abuse and violence in intimate relationships*, pp. 119-128 (chapter 6). Adelaide: Dulwich Centre Publications.

Waldegrave, C., Tamasese, K., Tuhaka, F. & Campbell, W. 2003: *Just Therapy – a journey: A collection of papers from the Just Therapy Team, New Zealand*. Adelaide: Dulwich Centre Publications.

Weingarten, K. 2003: *Common Shock: Witnessing violence every day - How we are harmed, how we can heal*. New York: Dutton.

White, M. 1995: 'Naming abuse and breaking free from its effects.' An interview by Christopher McLean in White, M., *Re- Authoring Lives: Interviews & essays*, pp. 82-111. Adelaide: Dulwich Centre Publications.

White, M. 2000: 'Re-engaging with history: the absent but implicit.' In White, M.: *Reflections on Narrative Practice: Essays & interviews*, pp. 35-58. Adelaide: Dulwich Centre Publications.

White, M. 2004: 'Working with people who are suffering the consequences of multiple trauma: A narrative perspective.' *International Journal of Narrative Therapy and Community Work*, 1:45-76.

CHAPTER TWO

Working with people who are suffering the consequences of multiple trauma:

A narrative perspective

by Michael White

This chapter places an emphasis on the priority given to the redevelopment and reinvigoration of a 'sense of myself' in working with people who have been subject to trauma. It describes how this can be achieved through the use of definitional ceremony structures, outsider-witness practices and re-authoring conversations. The last section of the chapter discusses the contribution of memory theorists and its relevance to work with people who have experienced trauma. More particularly it proposes that, in order to re-associate dissociated memory, we must first enable a revitalisation of the 'sense of myself'.

Introduction

There are many practices of narrative therapy that are relevant to work with people who have experienced trauma. These various narrative practices are employed to re-develop rich stories of people's lives and identities. Due to space constraints, I will only focus on a few of these narrative practices in this chapter – particularly those relating to 'definitional ceremony' structures, 'outsider-witness retellings', and 're-authoring conversations'. In a subsequent paper I intend to give a more detailed account of the relevance of these practices, and, as well, describe the application of other narrative practices in work with people who have been subject to trauma.

PART ONE
Value, resonance, and definitional ceremony

The effects of multiple trauma on a person's identity

In my work as a therapist, many of the people who are referred to me have experienced significant and recurrent trauma. Most of these people consult me about feelings of emptiness, desolation, and despair. They are often overwhelmed by a sense of hopelessness and paralysis, and believe that there is nothing whatsoever they can do to affect the shape of their life or the shape of events around them. Many of them have lost touch with a sense of personhood. They have lost touch with a particular and valued sense of who they are – a 'sense of myself'[1].

I'm sure that readers will be familiar with this 'sense of myself'. How many of you, when looking back at a stressful event and at how you responded in the context of this, have at times found yourself thinking, 'I know it was me, but I just wasn't myself'? One outcome of the experience of trauma is that people often lose touch with this familiar sense of their identity for an extended period of time.

Identity can be thought of as a 'territory' of life. When people experience trauma, and particularly when this is recurrent, there is a very significant shrinking of this territory of identity. When their territory of identity is so reduced, it becomes very difficult for people to know how to proceed in life; to know how to go forward with personal projects, to realise their plans for living. In these circumstances, all of the things in life that people usually give value to are diminished or reduced in presence and significance.

When a person has been through recurrent trauma, their 'sense of myself' can be so diminished it can become very difficult for them to give any account of what they give value to in life. This is because recurrent trauma is corrosive of what people hold precious in life. Recurrent trauma can have the effect of invalidating one's purposes in life and one's sentiments of living. Because of the effects of this corrosion and invalidation, when people have been through significant and recurrent trauma, it can be very difficult in therapeutic contexts for therapists to actually elicit what it is that these people give value to in their lives.

In my work with people who have been subject to multiple and recurrent trauma, one of the primary considerations is to restore that valued sense of who they are; the preferred sense of identity or personhood that in this chapter I will refer to as a 'sense of myself'. There are a number of key aspects to this restoration. One key aspect involves identifying what it is that people give value to in life. When this has been identified, the next task is to arrange therapeutic responses that are acknowledging and richly developing of this. Many practices of narrative therapy are well suited to this task.

This approach is nowhere more important than in circumstances when the therapist is being consulted by people who have experienced recurrent trauma that they have little or no memory of. In these circumstances, narrative practices can contribute to the reinvigoration of a 'sense of myself' which is continuous through past, present and future, and that provides a foundation for the development of an account of how people may have responded to the trauma they have been subject to. Apart from other things, this provides a foundation for a 're-association' of dissociated memory.

Doubly listening – seeking two stories

When working with people who've been through recurrent trauma, it's very important that therapists hear whatever it is that people want to share with them about the experience of trauma. To make this possible, therapy is clearly signified as a context in which people can speak about what may not have been previously spoken of[2]. However, at the same time, it's vitally important that the therapist listen for signs of what the person has continued to give value to in life despite all that they have been through, and for any expressions that might provide some hint of the person's *response* to trauma.

No-one is a passive recipient of trauma. People always take steps in endeavouring to prevent the trauma they are subject to, and, when preventing this trauma is clearly impossible, they take steps to try to modify it in some way or to modify its effects on their lives. These steps contribute to the preservation of, and are founded upon, what people hold precious. Even in the face of overwhelming trauma, people take steps to try to protect and to preserve what they give value to.

People's responses to trauma are based on what they give value to, on what they hold precious in life. However, in the context of trauma, and in its aftermath, these responses to trauma are often rendered invisible through diminishment and disqualification – these responses and what they signify in terms of what people give value to are regularly demeaned and ridiculed. Even when these responses to trauma are not disqualified in this way, they are often considered insignificant and are overlooked. This contributes to a sense of personal desolation, to the development of a sense of shame which is strongly experienced by so many people who have been subject to trauma, and to the erosion of a 'sense of myself'.

To summarise, in circumstances when people's very responses to the trauma they're going through, including the actions that they take to prevent it, to modify it, and to resist its effects, are disqualified or rendered irrelevant, the outcome is usually a sense of personal desolation and a strong sense of shame. In some circumstances this can develop into feelings of wretchedness and self-loathing.

In working with people who've been through trauma, it's very important that therapists not only hear whatever it is that is important for people to share about the experience of trauma and its consequences, but also initiate the sort of therapeutic inquiry that will provide people with an opportunity to identify their responses to the trauma they were put through. It is the rich description of these responses, and the acknowledgment of these, that contributes very significantly to the redevelopment of a preferred 'sense of myself'. This also provides a foundation for the re-association of dissociated memory, which will be discussed at the end of this chapter.

These responses to trauma - these steps that people take to try to prevent or to modify the trauma and its effects, these steps which have to do with efforts to hold onto and preserve what is precious to people despite trauma - are shaped by certain knowledges about life and skills of living. The steps that people take in the midst of trauma, and in its aftermath, that are invariably disqualified or diminished within the trauma context, are founded on knowledges of life and on skills of living that have been developed in the history of their lives, in the history of their relationships with others. Therapy can become a context in which these steps, and the knowledges and skill that they represent, can become known and profoundly acknowledged.

The knowledges that we develop about our lives have much to do with what we give value to. Whatever it is that we accord value to in life provides for us a purpose in living, a meaning for our lives, and a sense of how to proceed in life. What we accord value to in life is shaped by our relationships with others who have been significant to us – this can include family members, relatives, and friends – by our communities, by the institutions of these communities, and by our culture. And what we accord value to in life is often linked to notions about one's sentiment of living, one's ethics of existence, one's aesthetics of living and, at times, to specific spiritual notions. In identifying what people give value to, therapists have a foundation for the development of rich conversations that trace this into personal history, and that provide an account of how these knowledges of life and practices of living were generated. This establishes a fertile ground for the recovery and reinvigoration of the person's 'sense of myself', and for the development of an understanding of how the person responded to the trauma, and to its aftermath.

I use the term 'doubly listening' to describe my posture in these conversations. When meeting with people who are consulting me about trauma and its aftermath, I hear the story about the trauma, but I also hear expressions of what people have continued to accord value to in their lives despite what they have been through. As well, I find signs of the person's response to the trauma they went through. And I try to establish a context so that the multi-layered nature of those responses become richly known, powerfully acknowledged and honoured. When people first consult us about trauma and its consequences, they generally have very thin understandings of their responses to the trauma they have been subject to. In our therapeutic conversations with these people, their understanding of their own responses to trauma becomes richly known.

To reiterate, all of the therapeutic conversations that I have with people who have been through trauma are *double-storied* conversations, not single-storied. There is always the story about the trauma and its consequences – people have the opportunity to speak of their experiences of trauma, and they are actively supported in speaking about what hasn't been spoken of before. And, there is also the story about the person's response to trauma which is often very thinly known – this story is often only present as a very thin trace, one that can be highly difficult to identify. It is vitally important that we do get onto this trace, and that we assist people to thicken this up. The first step to achieving this is identifying what it is that people have continued to give value to despite everything they have been through.

I will now share a story of a therapeutic conversation that reflects this principle.

Julie's story

This is a story about a woman called Julie who had experienced recurrent abuse. Much of this abuse was perpetrated by her father, and by a neighbour, and she had been living with a man who reproduced this abuse. On numerous occasions Julie had tried to get free of the abusive context but has always returned to an unchanged violent situation to be subject to yet more trauma. Julie had a diagnosis of borderline personality disorder, experienced a pervasive sense of emptiness, and from time to time was overwhelmed by shame and despair. She had a history of cutting herself at these times.

Julie's usual escape route from the violence of the man she lived with was via a women's refuge. On the occasion of her most recent admission to this refuge, the workers there talked with Julie about her cycles of admissions to the refuge and about her cutting, and predicted that she would once again return to an unchanged violent situation unless something different was tried. They then asked Julie if she would agree to a meeting with me. She agreed to this, and an appointment was made for me to meet with Julie and with two of the refuge workers, Sally and Dianne, who had come to know her quite well over several years.

When I sat down and talked with Julie she told me that she had a borderline personality disorder, and that she mostly felt empty and desolate. She represented her life as a chronicle of tragic and demoralising events that occurred one after the after, events that seemed totally unrelated. Julie described herself as a passive recipient of these events. She had a sense that she could do nothing to shape their course; that there was no action that she could take to modify her circumstances in any way at all. In Julie's recounting of these events of her life, I detected no sense of personal agency, and no unifying 'sense of myself' that could be traced through these events.

After about forty minutes of listening to this chronicle of tragic and demoralising events, I checked with Julie if it would be okay for me to ask a question. She said that this would be okay. By this time I had some appreciation of the many tragic and traumatic experiences that she'd been through. One of her more recent painful experiences had occurred about eight months before our meeting. This was an experience of witnessing a child being run down by a motor car in the city. The child was seriously injured. There were other people at the scene who went to the child's assistance, and soon an ambulance arrived. Julie talked about how she had felt paralysed at this time. She found that she could not move, and was unable to assist at the accident scene. This experience of paralysis had clearly been significant to Julie, and although Julie did not say this, when she spoke of this paralysis I thought I detected a sense of shame. In all of the stories that I had heard from Julie, this was the only one in which I detected an expression of feeling, or affective tone.

In the space that I had negotiated to ask Julie a question, I inquired: 'When you were telling the story of the child being injured by a motor car, I sensed an expression of some significant feelings. Was this about relief that there were people present who were able to attend to the child, or was it about shame that you were unable to attend to the child yourself, or were these feelings about something else?" Julie said that she had never thought about it before, but that she supposed that it must have been shame – 'shame over letting the child down'. I wanted to know whether this was a mild shame or a moderate shame or a strong shame, hoping that Julie might judge this to be strong or at least moderate shame. After some reflection, Julie said that she thought it must have been strong shame, although she hadn't realised this at the time. I recall feeling quite enthusiastic about her conclusion that this was strong shame, because this indicated a significant opening for a conversation about what Julie gave value to in life.

I asked Julie why she would feel ashamed in this way. She said, 'Surely you would know?' I replied, 'Well, I live my life, not your life. I know about how and why I respond to situations, but I don't know how or why you respond to situations. So, I don't have a sense of what this event meant to you and why you would feel ashamed about this.' In response, Julie said, 'Well, I saw a child run down by a motor car. I should have done something to help this child, but I did nothing, and I think that I have lived with this shame ever since'. 'But why did your lack of action in this particular situation give rise to shame?' I asked. 'Can't you see' said Julie, 'there isn't anything in life that's worth much, but a child's life, that's different'. We discussed this further, and gradually Julie began to talk more openly about what she attributed value to. In the context of rendering her sense of shame more sensible to me, we both learned that she treasured children's lives.

Julie was actually quite surprised to hear herself speaking in this way about what she treasured. At this point I began to think about what sort of therapeutic inquiry would assist Julie to take this valuing of children's lives into a story-line of her life.

Finding an audience to what people value

The first step in this work with Julie was to discover what she gave value to. In my meetings with people who have been through very significant trauma it is not always easy to get onto this. In the context of trauma, what people give value to is often diminished, or totally disqualified. On account of this, people take measures to keep safe what is precious to them, and these measures usually involve secreting this away from others.

The second step in my work with Julie was to arrange for what was precious to her to be responded to in ways that would be highly acknowledging of this. A most powerful practice of acknowledgement involves the active participation of an audience. When I specifically recruit an audience to participate in therapeutic conversations, I refer to the members of this audience as 'outsider-witnesses' (see White 1995, 1997, 2000a; Russell & Carey 2003). This term 'outsider-witness' is borrowed from the field work of a North American cultural anthropologist called Barbara Myerhoff (1982, 1986). In the instance of my meeting with Julie, the two workers from the women's refuge, Sally and Dianne, were also in the room, listening to the interview as it progressed. These two women were to be the outsider witnesses. Having arrived at a point in our conversation at which Julie had spoken about what she significantly valued, I asked her to sit back, and to be an audience to my conversation with Sally and Dianne. I then began to interview Sally and Dianne about what they'd heard in Julie's story.

I had already introduced Sally and Dianne to the tradition of audience or 'outsider witness' response that I would be seeking from them. What is crucial is that the responses of the outsider witnesses are 'resonant' responses. It is not the role of the outsider witnesses to give an empathic response, to give advice, to express opinions, to make judgements, to point out strengths and resources, to praise, or to formulate interventions. Julie had been talking about what she gave value to – children's lives – and, in the outsider-witness retelling, it was the task of the two refuge workers to respond resonantly to this; for Sally and Dianne to re-present, in a rich and acknowledging way, what Julie gives value to in life.

In order to ensure that a 'resonant' response is generated in the retellings of the outsider witnesses, I leave very little to chance. Rather, I interview the outsider witnesses in the presence of the person whose life is at the centre of the retelling. This interview is shaped by four primary categories of inquiry.

Particularities of expressions

I began by asking Sally and Dianne what it was that they'd heard from Julie that had really caught their attention; that captured their imagination; that they were particularly drawn to; that struck a chord for them; that provided them with a sense of what it is that Julie accords value to.

In response, Sally and Dianne spoke of the story that Julie had told about not acting in relation to the child being injured, about the shame that she had experienced in relation to this. And they spoke in strong terms about what they had heard Julie giving value to – children's lives.

Julie was an audience to this conversation between me and the two refuge workers. It was very important that she was not in the conversation. The power of 'outsider-witness' responses is much greater when the person concerned is not in the conversation itself. In the position as an audience to the conversation between me and the refuge workers, Julie could hear what she would not have otherwise heard had she been in dialogue with Sally and Dianne.

Images of identity

I then asked Sally and Dianne to tell me what Julie's story had suggested to them about her; how it had affected their picture of her as a person; how it shaped their view of her; what it said to them about what might be important to Julie; and what it perhaps said about what she stood for in life, about what she believed in. Through questions like this, I was inviting the refuge workers to describe the images of Julie's identity that were evoked for them by the expressions they had been drawn to as they had listened to her story.

Sally and Dianne had been particularly drawn to the account of what Julie gave value to in life, about what was precious to her, and, in response to my questions, began to speak about the sorts of images of Julie's life and identity that this evoked for them. As they spoke about these images, I encouraged them to speculate about what these implied about Julie's purposes, values, beliefs, hopes, dreams and commitments. Amongst other things, Sally and Dianne presented images of a caring and protective adult, of a person who had a strong desire to go the extra mile in supporting someone more vulnerable than herself.

Throughout this time, Sally and Dianne were talking to me about Julie. They were not talking directly to Julie. They did not turn to Julie and say, 'Julie, when you said this, this is what came to me'. Instead they said, 'When I heard this from Julie, this is what it evoked for me ...' This process of retelling in which Julie was strictly in the audience position was very powerfully authenticating of what Julie accorded value to. Had Sally and Dianne turned to Julie and said directly to her: 'Look, it's really important that you treasure this value that you give to children's lives, and that you hold onto this', this would make little, if any, difference to Julie. This could too easily be discounted, and would not provide, for Julie, that experience of resonance in the outside world.

Embodying their interest

It is not possible to listen to the significant stories of other people's lives without these touching us, without these affecting us personally in some way. And it is not by chance that we become engaged by particular aspects of people's stories. Julie's account of shame and of what she accorded value to in life struck a chord for Sally and Dianne. And the images of Julie's identity which were evoked by her expressions, and which Sally and Dianne had the opportunity to speak of, had set off reverberations down into the history of their own lives. These reverberations touched on specific experiences of their personal histories, which had come into memory, and had lit up for them.

I asked Sally and Dianne about why they were drawn to particular expressions of Julie's story, and about what these images of Julie's identity had struck a chord with in their own personal histories. In response, Sally spoke about how she had two children, and of how Julie's statements about the value of a child's life had her thinking even more about what her own children's lives mean to her, and about some of the ways in which her own life was different for having these children. Dianne spoke about some of her experiences as a child. She had known some adults who had not treasured children's lives in any way, and she had known one or two who had. She spoke poignantly about what a difference it had made to her to know these adults who cared for children, and what a difference it had specifically made for her.

As Sally and Dianne spoke of these personal resonances, it became clear to Julie that their interest in her life was not simply academic or professional interest, but personal interest. As Sally and Dianne situated their interest in Julie's expressions in the history of their own experiences of life, this interest became embodied interest, not disembodied interest. And to embody one's interest in this way is powerfully authenticating of it.

Acknowledging catharsis

When the stories of people's lives touch on the history of our own experiences in ways that trigger resonances, we are inevitably moved by this. Here I am not just referring to being moved emotionally, but about being moved in the broad sense of this word – about where this experience has taken us in our own thoughts; in terms of our reflections on our own existence; in terms of our understandings of our own lives; in terms of speculation about conversations that we might have with others; or in terms of options for action in the world – for example, in regard to repossessing what we find precious in our own histories, or in regard to addressing current predicaments in our own lives and relationships.

I began to interview Sally and Dianne about their experience of movement in this broader sense of the word. Dianne responded with: 'Well, on account of what I've heard from Julie, I have a new understanding of how I got through some of the things I had to deal with as a child and as a young woman. Right now I am much more in touch with the ways in which I was helped through some really bad times by a couple of adults who cared about me. One of these people was a neighbour, and another was our local grocer. And this has given me an idea about reconnecting with these people, to talk to them about what they meant to me. I think that this will be an important step for me to take, because I am sure that it will give me a sense of having a fuller life'. Sally spoke about her relationships with her children: 'As Julie was speaking, I thought more and more about the lives of my two children. I have felt more honouring of my wish for my children to have contact with adults who treasure children's lives. I feel that I have been putting up with some circumstances that have had me breaking my promise to myself on this. I don't want my children to have to spend time with adults who don't value them properly. So, because of Julie's story I am going to make some decisions about my children's contact with some members of my extended family, decisions that I have been putting off'.

In the context of this acknowledgement of movement, Julie was put in touch with the fact that the ripples of her story were touching the lives of these other two women, taking them to another place in their lives that was important to them. In this context, Julie experienced making a significant contribution to the lives of others. I do not know of any therapeutic practice that is more powerfully acknowledging than this. I could meet with Julie every day of her life in an effort to help her to appreciate that she is a worthwhile person. But this would make little, if any, difference to her sense of self. In fact, this could even have the effect of alienating me from her. But to experience outsider witnesses acknowledging movement in their own lives in this way on account of one's story is invariably extraordinarily validating and potentially restorative. It is potentially restorative of the sort of 'sense of myself' that Julie has found to be so fleeting in the history of her own life.

Another way of thinking about this fourth part of the outsider-witness retelling is to link it to the idea of 'catharsis'. In contemporary times, catharsis is often associated with the idea that, on account of historical trauma or whatever, there are substances like pain held under pressure in the emotional system, in much the same way that a head of steam is held under pressure in a steam engine. This is associated with the notion that healing is the outcome of the discharge or release of these substances. I am not very fond of this modern version of catharsis. I'm much more interested in the central classical understanding of catharsis. For the ancient Greeks catharsis meant many things, but its central meaning was linked to the performance of Greek Tragedy. The performance of Greek Tragedy was cathartic for the audience if it moved them to another place in their lives; if it provided the impetus for the members of the audience to become other than who they were at the outset of the performance. If, on account of witnessing this powerful drama, the people in the audience could think differently about their life, or if they had a new perspective on their own personal history, or if they became newly engaged with certain precious values and beliefs, or if they had new ideas about how they might proceed in life, ways that were more in harmony with these values and beliefs, this was understood to be a cathartic experience.

Extending this metaphor to the therapy realm, when I interviewed Sally and Dianne about movement in their own lives, they acknowledged catharsis. They spoke about what it was about Julie's story that had touched their own lives in ways that would make a difference. I have already talked of the potential significance, to Julie, of witnessing this acknowledgement of catharsis, and I will again refer to this. Can you imagine how powerful this was for Julie, who had so totally believed that the world would never respond to the fact of her existence? Can you imagine how this might affect a woman who thoroughly believed that she could never be influential in any positive way in the lives of others? Can you imagine what witnessing this acknowledgement of catharsis might do for a woman who had no sense of personal agency? And can you imagine the part that this might play in restoring and further developing that 'sense of myself' that had been so elusive in the history of Julie's life?

When I had finished interviewing Sally and Diane I turned to Julie and asked her a series of questions about what she had heard. In this interview, I did not encourage Julie to reproduce the entire content of what the outsider witnesses had said. Rather, the interview was shaped by the same four categories of inquiry that structured my interview of Sally and Dianne, who were the outsider witnesses for our meeting. First, I wanted to know what Julie had heard that had struck a chord for her; about what she had been specifically drawn to; about the particularities of what had caught her attention or captured her imagination: 'What did you hear that you were drawn to? Were there particular words that struck a chord for you?' etc.

Second, I interviewed Julie about the metaphors or the mental pictures of her own life that were evoked by the retelling of the outsider witnesses: 'As you listened, what images of life came to mind? Did you have any realisations about your own life? How did this affect your picture of who you are as a person?' etc. At this time I also interviewed Julie about what these images might reflect about her identity: 'What did this say to you about what is important to you, about what you treasure? What does this suggest about your purposes in life? Do you have a sense of what this reflects about what you stand for, or about your hopes in life?' etc.

Third, I interviewed Julie about her sense of why it was that she could relate to what she'd heard in the outsider-witness retellings. This encouraged her to identify those aspects of her personal experience that resonated with what she had been drawn to in the responses of Sally and Dianne: 'You have spoken about what you heard that struck a chord for you. What did this strike a chord with in terms of your own experiences of life? What did it touch on in regard to your own history? Did particular memories light up at this time? Did anything else become more visible to you about your own personal experiences that would explain why you were so drawn to what you heard?' etc.

Finally I asked Julie questions that provided her with an opportunity to identify and to express catharsis; that provided her with a frame for speaking about where the responses of the outsider witnesses, and her reflections upon these responses, had moved her to: 'What is your sense of where these conversations have taken you? What is the place that you are in right now that you were not in at the beginning of these conversations? You have talked of some important realisations about your life, realisations that were triggered while listening to Sally and Diane, and I would be interested in your predictions about the possible effects of these realisations. You have also given voice to some significant conclusions regarding what your life is about, and I would be interested to know if this has contributed to any new understandings about your own history ...' etc.

Definitional ceremony structure – tellings and re-tellings

This therapeutic process that I have outlined I define as 'definitional ceremony'. The definitional ceremony metaphor shapes structured levels of tellings and retellings, and narrative practices that reproduce a specific tradition of acknowledgement. I believe that definitional ceremony is an apt metaphor to describe this feature of narrative practice, for it creates what I consider to be a ceremony for the re-definition of people's identity. I believe that this fits with the original sentiment associated with this metaphor, which I drew from the work of Barbara Myerhoff, a North American cultural anthropologist (1982, 1986).

As illustrated in my account of my conversations with Julie, Sally, and Dianne, the definitional ceremonies of narrative practice always consist of at least three parts.

i) *The telling*

    In the example that I have given, I first interviewed Julie in ways that facilitated a double-storied telling. This was a telling of stories of tragedy and trauma, and also of Julie's response to tragedy and trauma in ways that made visible what she gave value to in life. In these interviews, the therapist always provides, through appropriate questions, a context for a double-storied telling. At this time the outsider witnesses were strictly in the audience position. I believe that 'outsider witness' is an appropriate term with which to describe the members of the audience, for, at this time, they are not active participants in the conversation, but are witnessing this conversation from the outside.

ii) *The re-telling of the telling*

    When Julie's double-storied telling had developed to the point that there was some clarity about what she accorded value to in life, I arranged for an external response. This was an external response that, amongst other things, was powerfully resonant with what Julie accorded value to in life. This resonant response was the outcome of my interview of the Sally and Dianne who were present as outsider witnesses. In this response, these outsider witnesses engaged in a vivid re-presentation of what it was that Julie accorded value to. At this time Julie was strictly in the audience position, listening to the responses of the outsider witnesses as I interviewed them about what they had been drawn to (the expression), about the metaphors and mental pictures that this had evoked (the image), about what this had resonated with in terms of their own personal experience (embodiment), and about the ways in which this had moved them (catharsis).

I was active in the structuring of the outsider-witness retelling. I didn't simply ask Sally and Dianne: 'Well, what do you think of what Julie said?' Instead, I carefully interviewed them according to the four categories of enquiry I have already described. I will again emphasise the important responsibility that the therapist has in scaffolding this interview through these four categories of inquiry. Common expressions of empathy, like 'I feel deeply for Julie on account of the fact that ...' will rarely achieve a powerfully resonant re-presentation of what the person gives value to. And, as I have previously mentioned in this chapter, practices associated with proposing advice, offering opinions, giving affirmations, or pointing out positives are unlikely to be successful in establishing this resonance, and can be hazardous in these contexts.

It is important that this responsibility for the scaffolding of the outsider-witness retelling is exercised from the outset of these definitional ceremonies. For example, if an outsider witness was to commence their retelling in the superlative (for example, 'Well, I think Julie is just amazing because ...') it would be up to the therapist to quickly respond with a question that encouraged this outsider witness to provide some account of the particular aspects of Julie's telling that s/he was drawn to (for example: 'Julie's story was obviously very engaging of you. What was it exactly that you heard or witnessed that caught your attention, and that might be really significant to Julie?').

iii) The re-telling of the re-telling

Following part one (the telling) and part two (the re-telling of telling) of the definitional ceremony structure, I interviewed Julie again, this time about her response to what she had heard from the outsider witnesses. I refer to this third part of the definitional ceremony as 'the retelling of the retelling', and, as I have described, this is informed by the same four categories of inquiry that shape the outsider-witness retelling: by inquiry into a) the particularities of expressions of the outsider witnesses that gained the person's attention, b) the images of the person's life and identity that were evoked by these expressions, c) the personal resonances that these expressions touched on, and d) the person's experience of catharsis. At this time the outsider witnesses are again occupying the audience position. Within these definitional ceremonies, all the shifts between the three stages are distinct and relatively formal movements. If these distinct movements were to degenerate, and the conversations become simple dialogue between the various parties rather than structured tellings and retellings, it is highly unlikely that this would enable the redevelopment and reinvigoration of the 'sense of myself' that is vital in addressing the effects of trauma and it's consequences.

Summary

At the outset of the definitional ceremony, Julie had very thin conclusions about her life and identity. There was virtually no trace of the 'sense of myself' that is founded upon an experience of the continuity of precious themes through the history, present, and future of one's life, and which provides a foundation for the experience of personal intimacy, and for intimate relationships with others. On account of this, Julie's predominant feelings were of desolation, emptiness, incompetence, and worthlessness.

Identifying what Julie accorded value to in life, and establishing a context for a strongly resonant response to this through outsider-witness retellings, were the first steps in the redevelopment and reinvigoration of Julie's 'sense of myself'. The significance of these opening steps were attested to by the richness of Julie's retelling of the outsider-witness responses, and also by her description of some of the bodily sensations that these gave rise to: 'As I was listening I was having these unusual feelings. I don't really know how to describe these feelings. I am bit stuck for words right now. But it's like something ... well perhaps it is like starting to come out of some sort of deep freeze. Yes, that's it ... maybe it's like coming out of a hibernation.'

Outsider-witness sources

These definitional ceremonies of narrative practice always engage outsider witnesses. In the example given here, these outsider witnesses were known to Julie. Often this is the case – the person has a pre-existing connection with the people who are invited to participate as outsider witnesses (for example, these people might be relatives, friends, acquaintances, or, as in Julie's case, members of the professional disciplines who the person has come to know). However, it is not always the case that the person will have this already established connection with the people who are invited to participate as outsider witnesses. At times the outsider witnesses to my work with people who consult me about the consequences of trauma are drawn from a pool of volunteers who have insider knowledge of trauma and its effects. Often these volunteers come from a list of names of people who have consulted me about the consequences of trauma in their own lives, and who have been enthusiastic about joining me in my work with others who are following in their footsteps[3]. At other times these outsider witness are drawn from my own personal and social network, or from people of the professional disciplines who are colleagues or who are visiting Dulwich Centre for training and consultation.

Regardless of the source of outsider witnesses, I always do my best to observe my responsibility for the shape of the outsider-witness retelling. In the observance of this responsibility, I actively interview the outsider witnesses, and this interview is shaped by the four categories of inquiry that I have outlined in this presentation. When the outside witnesses are drawn from the professional disciplines, it is usually important to have conversations about the nature of the tradition of acknowledgement that is reproduced in the outsider-witness retellings. This assists these workers to step back from traditions of theorising and hypothesising about people's lives and relationships; from evaluating people's expressions according to the expert knowledges of the professional disciplines; and from formulating interventions and treatments for the problems of people's lives. These conversations about the tradition of outsider-witness retellings open space for members of the professional disciplines to maintain:

a) an awareness of what it is that they are drawn to in people's expressions,

b) a consciousness of the images that are evoked for them by these expressions,

c) an attentiveness to what it is in their own experience that resonates with these expressions and images, and

d) a reflective stance on the ways that they are moved on account of being an audience to these tellings, and on account of participating in these retellings.

The extended performance of catharsis

In this chapter I have placed considerable emphasis on the significance of the acknowledgement of catharsis on behalf of outsider witnesses. In doing this, I have provided an account of how outsider witnesses might acknowledge catharsis in the second stage of the definitional ceremony. I would now like to describe options for the extended performance of catharsis.

People who have been through significant and recurrent trauma usually have a strong sense that the world is totally unresponsive to the fact of their existence. Further, their sense of personal agency is often diminished to the point that they do not believe that it is possible for them to influence the world around them in any way. The outcome of this is a sense of the irrelevance of one's life, of emptiness, and of personal paralysis – a sense of one's life being frozen in time. On account of this, it is particularly important for people who have been subject to trauma to experience a world that is in some way responsive to the fact of their existence, and to experience making at least a small difference in this world. The extended performance of catharsis has the potential to contribute significantly to this achievement.

I will now share a story that illustrates this potential:

Marianne had a history of significant and recurrent trauma. As an outcome of this, amongst other things, she'd had a long struggle with the consequences of what is usually referred to as dissociated memory: under stressful circumstances she was prone to re-living the trauma of her history without having any awareness at the time that these were memories that she was re-experiencing. In our second meeting I had interviewed Marianne in the presence of three outsider witnesses. Two of these were people who'd previously consulted me about the effects of trauma in their lives, and at the end of our work together had been delighted about their names being entered into one of my outsider-witness registers. The other outsider witness was a woman called Hazel, who was a counsellor. Hazel had a special interest in working with people who had been subject to trauma.

At the outset of our meeting I had interviewed Marianne about some of her experience of trauma, and the consequences of this to her life. Through careful listening during this stage of our meeting, I had also found a gateway to explore some of her responses to trauma, and the foundation of these responses – what it was that she gave value to in her life. I then interviewed the outsider witnesses according to the manner that I have been describing in this presentation, and noted that Marianne seemed particularly drawn to Hazel's acknowledgement of catharsis. In this acknowledgement, Hazel had spoken of some new realisations that she'd had about what might be helpful in her work with two of her clients. These clients were both women who were consulting Hazel about the effects on trauma on their lives. Hazel said that until this moment she had felt somehow constrained in her work with these two women, and frustrated that she couldn't find a way of proceeding that was to her satisfaction. She also said that over the last month or so she had become concerned that she was failing these two women.

In the context of the outsider-witness retelling, Hazel spoke of these new realisations, of the possibilities that she thought these might bring to her therapeutic conversations with these two women who were consulting her. She rounded off this acknowledgement of catharsis with: 'Because of what I've heard from Marianne, I now have some clear ideas about how to proceed in my work with my clients'. When I interviewed Marianne about her response to the retellings of the outsider witnesses, she dwelt for some time on this account of her contribution to Hazel's work. She seemed a little awestruck: 'I always think of myself as something that is useless, and just a burden to others. Who would have ever thought that I could do anything that might help someone else. This is a big thing to get my head around, it really is. It is going to take a while!'

At the end of this meeting Hazel was acutely aware of the significance, to Marianne, of her acknowledgement of catharsis. Three weeks later I received two letters, addressed to Marianne via my office, along with a covering note from Hazel. In this covering note Hazel explained that these two letters had been co-written by her and her two clients, and that these letters provided an account of the ways in which Marianne's story had opened new avenues for these women to address the consequences of trauma in their lives. In the covering note, Hazel suggested that I read these letters to Marianne on the occasion of my next meeting with her.

This I subsequently did, and Marianne was so moved by this that, on two occasions, she had to take time out over a cigarette in our courtyard in order to, in her words, 'Get herself together again'. She was also powerfully touched by the gifts that we had discovered in the two envelopes. One of these letters was accompanied by a beautiful hand-crafted card with an inscription that was honouring of Marianne's contribution. The other letter was accompanied by five coupons for espresso and cake at a city café. This card and these coupons were a gift from these two women, who had in writing acknowledged Marianne's contribution to their efforts to heal from the traumas of their lives.

These letters, card and coupons represent an example of the extended performance of catharsis. The extended performance of catharsis is about post-session initiatives that are taken by outsider witnesses in following up acknowledgements of catharsis made in the second stage of a definitional ceremony. It is this extended performance of catharsis that provided for Julie an unmistakable sense of personal agency, and a sense of the world being responsive to the fact of her existence. In this way, the extended performance of catharsis has the potential to very significantly contribute to the redevelopment and reinvigoration of the 'sense of myself' that I have referred to in this presentation. Amongst other things, in response to reading these letters and receiving these gifts, Marianne spoke of bodily sensations very similar to those reported by Julie.

As I have mentioned, Marianne was quite overwhelmed by these acknowledgements. Some time later she told me that she had never experienced anything even close to this sort of acknowledgement in her entire life; that this was 'light years' away from anything that she'd ever known. At this time she also said that it had been important that this acknowledgment wasn't in a form that she could refute or deny. She hadn't experienced this acknowledgement as an attempt to point out positives in the hope of making her feel better, but as a factual account of the ripples which had their genesis in her own expressions, and which had touched the life of others in significant ways. This provided her with a platform for new initiatives in her own life to recover from the trauma of her own history.

I later learned that this extended performance of catharsis had established a profoundly healing resonance for Marianne. The realisation that she had contributed to possibilities for others in addressing injustice had resonated with a long held but faintly known secret hope – that all she had been through would not be for nothing. This news did not surprise me, for I have found that it is common for people who have been subject to significant trauma to hold onto a longing for the world to be different on account of what they have been through; or a secret hope that all they have been through, all they have endured, wasn't for nothing; or a hidden desire to contribute to the lives of others who have had similar experiences; or a fantasy about playing some part in relieving the suffering of others; or perhaps a passion to play some part in acts of redress in relation to the injustices of the world.

The value of definitional ceremony structures

In this chapter I have been focusing on the place of the definitional ceremony structure in work with people who have been subject to trauma. I cannot emphasise strongly enough the effectiveness of this structure. It has the potential to very significantly contribute to the reinvigoration of that 'sense of myself' that is so often diminished and even erased by experiences of trauma. In my experience, there is no therapeutic process that has more powerful effects in such circumstances. Perhaps the easiest way for me to convey this is to share another story.

Paul

Paul, a twelve-year old boy, was brought to see me by his mother and father, who were highly concerned about him. According to them, he was persistently sad, apprehensive and lonely, and, in a variety of ways, had been expressing highly negative thoughts about his identity and about his life. As these parents described their concerns to me, Paul was silently crying.

According to these parents, Paul had always been a sensitive boy who had a habit of taking things to heart. It hadn't been uncommon for him to be distressed about many of the trails and tribulations of his childhood, but over the past eighteen months his parents had noticed the development of a more general apprehensiveness and sadness that was now touching virtually every aspect of his existence.

Paul was still crying, so I asked his parents some questions about what they understood to be the context of this development. Amongst other things, Paul's mother spoke of the incessant teasing and bullying that he had been subject to at school in recent times. At this juncture Paul began to sob, and I took this to be confirmation of his mother's observation about the significance of this teasing and bullying.

I turned to consult Paul about this, but he made it clear that he wasn't yet ready to join our conversation. I asked him if it would be okay for me to interview his parents about their further understanding of this teasing, and the effects of this on his life, and he signalled that this would be okay. I then initiated a conversation with these parents about what they knew about the specific tactics of this teasing, about the attitudes that were expressed in this, and about what they understood to be the consequences of this to Paul's life.

For example, I inquired about their understanding of how these tactics and attitudes were affecting Paul's image of himself as a person, and about what they were talking him into about his life. I also inquired about their understanding of how these tactics were interfering with his social and emotional worlds. It seemed quite clear that these were isolating Paul, and highly disturbing his emotional life. It was at this point that, for the first time, his mother declared that it was 'abuse' that Paul was being subjected to.

Paul now seemed more ready to enter the conversation. In response to my inquiry, he confirmed his parents' speculation about his sadness and loneliness, and about the negative conclusions that he held about his identity and his life; that he was 'weak', 'pathetic', 'inadequate' and 'incompetent'. He also confirmed their understandings about the principle context of these experiences – incessant teasing and frequent bullying at school. I was openly curious about how Paul had been able to enter our conversation. I wondered aloud whether it was his parents' naming of the tactics of peer abuse, the naming of the attitudes expressed in these tactics, and/or their understandings of the consequences of these to his life, that had something to do with this. Paul confirmed that it was all of this, and as our conversation developed I learned that this was the first occasion upon which these tactics, attitudes, and their consequences had been named in their particularities. It was clear that this had provided him with some relief.

In response to initiating a conversation about the action that this family had taken in their efforts to address these circumstances, I learned that Paul's mother had endeavoured to take this up with school authorities on several occasions, but to no avail. Each time her concerns had been dismissed with versions of: 'We have looked into this, and believe that the problem resides principally with Paul. He clearly needs some assistance with his self-esteem' and 'Don't you think it is about time that Paul looked at himself. It is a big world out there, and he is just going to have to learn to be more assertive'.

After further conversation about the actions taken by the parents based on this understanding of the circumstances of Paul's predicament, I initiated an inquiry into Paul's responses to what he was being subjected to. It is my understanding that no-one is a passive recipient of the abuses that are perpetrated on their lives. All people respond to what they are being put through and continue to respond, although it is usually the case that they are mostly unfamiliar with these responses. This is because, in the context of abuse, these responses are mostly discouraged, diminished, ridiculed and demeaned, and invariably go unrecognised and unacknowledged. It is my understanding that people's responses to abuse are founded upon what it is that they give value to in their lives, and upon ways of relating that can be understood as practices of counter-power.

In any conversation with people who have been subject to abuse, I believe it to be of critical importance to render visible and to unpack their responses to what they have been put through. It is in this unpacking of their responses that what it is that people give value to can become richly known. It is in this unpacking that the practices of counter-power can be appreciated in their particularities, and further elaborated. And it is this unpacking that provides a foundation for the further development of these practices of counter-power. In the usual run of life, it is very rare for the development and performance of these practices of counter-power to be significantly acknowledged, despite the fact that this achievement reflects the attainment of quite extraordinary social skills[4].

As an outcome of this inquiry into Paul's responses to what he was being put through, we discovered that, amongst other things, he had taken steps to befriend the school librarian so that he could spend lunch times in the school library, away from the culture of the schoolyard. This and other initiatives were unpacked in our conversation. As an upshot of this, Paul and his parents became much more familiar with the particularities of the practices of counter-power that Paul had been developing, with the roots of these, and with what these initiatives reflected about what he accorded value to in life. It was readily apparent that Paul was finding further comfort in this evolving conversation in which the particularities of his responses to trauma were becoming more richly known.

With the approval of Paul and his parents, I called the school. It was my hope that some collaboration with the relevant school authorities might contribute to general initiatives in addressing those aspects of the culture of the schoolyard that were abusive, and to specific initiatives in response to

Paul's experience of this abuse. I had also hoped that it might be possible for me to meet with the children who were perpetrating the peer abuse. The school's response to my overture confirmed the prediction of Paul's mother – it was not positive. Despite the care that I took, the school principal was clearly annoyed with my approach, and demanded to know: 'What are these allegations about the culture of the schoolyard?'

I called Paul's family and spoke to his mother about a substitute plan – to invite to our next meeting some other children, strangers to Paul, who had insider experience of peer abuse. I suggested that these children might appreciate aspects of Paul's story that might be lost to us as adults, and that their responses might provide Paul with the sort of validation that was beyond our ability to provide. Paul's mother was enthusiastic about this idea, as, apart from other things, Paul's acute loneliness had been such a source of concern to her. Paul's father's response was: 'Well, I guess we've got nothing to lose!' Paul felt positive about the idea, although he was somewhat apprehensive about it.

In the context of therapeutic practice, it is not uncommon for me to refer to my registers – these are lists of names and contact details of people who have consulted me in the past and who have volunteered to contribute to my work with people who follow in their footsteps. So, from my register of the names of children who had been referred to me in relation to the consequences of peer abuse in their lives, I called the families of the three most recent volunteers. I did not need to proceed up the list, as all of these children were enthusiastic about this summons, as were their parents. Before long I was meeting with Paul and his parents, and these three guests.

At the outset of this meeting, I interviewed Paul about his experiences of peer abuse, about what he had learned about the specific tactics of peer abuse that he had been subject to, about the consequences of this to his life, and about his responses to what he had been put through. I scaffolded this conversation in a way that provided Paul with an opportunity to thickly describe the counter-practices that he had engaged in, and what it was that he had continued to give value to in his life, and had refused to surrender. During this first part of our meeting, our three guests were strictly an audience to our conversation.

I then asked Paul and his parents to sit back, and began to interview these children about:

a) what they had heard from Paul that had particularly captured their attention;

b) the mental pictures and metaphors that this had evoked, and what this suggested to them about who Paul was as a person and about what was important to him;

c) why they could relate to what they were hearing; about what this struck a chord with in their own experience; and about

d) where they had personally journeyed to on account of being present as witnesses to Paul's story about abuse, and on account of his responses to this.

It was in the context of this retelling by these children that Paul's contribution to the development of the practices of counter-power became more visible, and what Paul stood for in life became more richly known: 'Paul didn't let himself get caught up in all of this. Nothing that these kids did could get him to join in with them in this teasing and bullying'; 'Paul stands for more caring and understanding ways'; 'Paul is one of those kids who won't pass the buck. He didn't find smaller kids to pass this bullying on to.'

As the retelling of these three children evolved, Paul began to cry, and then sob. It was my guess that this was significantly an outcome of the fact that the very ways of being in life that had been so demeaned and disqualified in the context of peer abuse were now being acknowledged and honoured. It was also my guess that, on account of this, Paul was separating from all of the negative conclusions that had been imposed on his identity in the context of peer abuse. When it came time for our three outsider witnesses to sit back, and for me to interview Paul about what he had heard in this retelling, and about where this had taken him to in regard to realisations about his own life, he confirmed my hunch. The experience of this retelling did turn out to be a turning-point in his life, and I gained a strong sense that he would never again be vulnerable to these negative conclusions about his identity and his life.

I should say that these three children did a great job in acknowledging the ways in which Paul's story, and the opportunity afforded in their retelling of his story, was transporting of them. In acknowledging the transporting aspects of these experiences, these children talked about, amongst other things, possible action that might be taken by them that might further contribute to some redress in relation to the injustices of peer abuse. This acknowledgement of the transporting aspects of these experiences is invariably highly resonant for people who have experienced abuse. This is resonant with a range of sentiments of life, including a longing for the world to be different on account of what they have been through.

There is more to the story of my conversations with Paul, his parents, and the three children who joined as outsider witnesses for three of these conversations. I will just say a little of one of the developments that unfolded during the course of our meetings, and that I considered to be outstanding. I learned in my fifth meeting that Paul had begun to make it his business to seek out other children who had insider knowledge of peer abuse. Most of these children were from his school. Upon identifying these children, he was engaging them in conversations about what being subject to peer abuse reflected about what was important to them, and about what they stood for in life; that is, more honourable ways of being boys in the culture of the schoolyard. As well, because the identification and appreciation of his own responses to peer abuse as practices of counter-power had been very significant to Paul, he was inviting stories from these other children about their own responses to what they had been put through. This was contributing to the development of a shared stock of knowledge about the practices of counter-power, and to initiatives in the development of an alternative culture of the schoolyard. At a subsequent meeting I had the great pleasure of meeting with Paul and several of these children.

Later, at the end of our series of meetings, I asked Paul and his parents to reflect on our meetings, and to talk with me about what they had found most useful, and about their understandings of this. I also wanted to know about anything that they had found unhelpful. In response to these questions, they spoke a lot about our meetings when the three other boys were present as outsider witnesses. I asked what value they attributed to these meetings in our overall work together: 'Was their contribution worth an extra meeting? Like an extra therapy session? Or was it worth half a therapy session, or two therapy sessions? What is your sense of this?' In response to my question, Paul and his parents all gave me their individual estimations. These were all high. I divided these figures by three to get the average, which turned out to be 837.4 sessions. My contribution to the therapy was six; I'd had six meetings with this family. So of the 843.4 sessions of therapy that it had taken to address the trauma that Paul was being subject to, my contribution was less that 1%. This is not an exemplary example of the outcome of employing the definitional ceremony structure in our work with people who consult us about experiences of trauma. People routinely value the responses of outsider witnesses very highly when these responses are shaped according to the tradition of acknowledgement that I have been describing in this presentation.

I have offered here three examples of the employment of the definitional ceremony structure in work with people who have been subject to trauma. In all of these examples, with Julie, Marianne and Paul, the outsider witnesses achieved something that was beyond my ability to achieve. However, I was nonetheless influential in all of these examples – these outsider-witness responses would not have taken the shape that they took if I hadn't actively interviewed the outsider witnesses according to the four categories of inquiry that I have outlined in different places in this chapter. I believe that it was the act of interviewing the outsider witnesses according to these categories of inquiry that facilitated retellings that were so strongly resonant for Julie, Marianne, and for Paul.

PART TWO
Re-authoring conversations:
From a single-storied to a multi-storied existence

I will now review a subject that I touched on earlier when describing the principle of listening doubly. This subject is the multi-storied nature of life.

At first contact, people who have been through trauma do their best to explain the sorry and painful predicaments that they find their lives to be in. In this explanation they link some of the events of their lives in a sequence unfolding through time according to specific themes that are usually of tragedy and loss. Although these explanations are often quite thin and disjointed, and usually exclude any account of the sort of valued themes that are reflected in a preferred 'sense of myself', these explanations nonetheless constitute stories.

In these circumstances, people take these stories to represent the totality of their existence; people experience their lives to be single storied, perceiving themselves trapped in a single dimension of living, one that predominantly features a sense of hopelessness, futility, emptiness, shame, despair and depression. And yet, life is invariably multi-storied. In order to draw out the implications of this understanding about the multi-storied nature of life, it can be useful to consider a building metaphor. According to this metaphor, life is represented as a multi-storied building without elevators, stairwells, escalators, and fire escapes. On account of this, there is no way for the people who are restricted to the ground floor to get access to the other floors. These people are denied access to the other floors of this multi-storied building of life; they are denied access to these other territories of living in which there are to be found many things precious about their lives, including other knowledges of life and practices of living that could assist them to find a way out of their predicaments of life, that could assist in their efforts to heal from the trauma they have been subject to.

In further considerations of the relevance of this building metaphor, we can conceive of narrative practices, including those associated with definitional ceremony, as providing the scaffolding for the development of therapeutic conversations just as construction workers rely upon the arrangement of scaffolding to facilitate their construction work. It is in the building of this scaffold through the structures and questions of therapeutic inquiry that therapists make it possible for people to get access to the other stories of their lives, and to the other territories of identity that are associated with these stories. Within the context of therapeutic conversations, upon first identifying these other stories and territories of existence, these can seem miniscule.

To risk the hazards of mixing metaphors, in the first place, these other territories of existence can be likened to atolls existing in the expanse of a sea of relentless currents and of frequent storms. However, as these alternative stories are further developed in therapeutic conversations, they become islands upon which safety and sustenance can be found, then archipelagos, and eventually continents of security that open other worlds of life to the people who are consulting us. In the development of these alternative stories, in the exploration of these other territories of life, people's stories of trauma and pain are not invalidated or displaced. However, people find that, as an outcome of these conversations, they have another place in which to stand that makes it possible for them to give expression to their experiences of trauma without being defined by these experiences.

In the illustrations that I have given in this chapter, the first step in accessing these alternative territories of life was through the discovery of what it is that people give value to. People always accord value to something. Even the mere fact of a person's continued existence is evidence of this. Although what it is that people accord value to can be very difficult to identify, people's expressions of pain and distress usually provide some clue to this. For example, a person's expression of pain can be considered a testimony to what it is that the person gives value to that was violated or dishonoured in the context of trauma. According to this understanding, the intensity of the pain corresponds with the intensity to which the person held precious what was violated or dishonoured. And the experience of day-to-day distress as an outcome of trauma can be considered a reflection of the extent to which a person is committed to maintaining a relationship with what they give value to, of the extent to which a person has refused to become resigned to aspects of their experiences of life, of their situation, and of their circumstance (White 2000b, 2003). Ongoing day-to-day distress as an outcome of trauma can be understood to be a tribute to the maintenance of an ongoing relationship with what a person holds precious, and a refusal to surrender this.

To reiterate, the identification of what people give value to opens the door to the further development of the alternative stories of people's lives, and to explorations of the other territories of people's identity. In each of the illustrations given in this chapter, the next step in the further development of these stories, in the opening of these territories, was to arrange for highly resonant responses to what people give value to. In these responses, what people give value to was re-presented in ways that contributed to the rich description of this, and in ways that were highly acknowledging and authenticating of this.

In the next section of this chapter, I will focus on the ways in which re-authoring conversations can be employed in the further development of the alternative stories of people's lives, and in the mapping of the alternative territories of their identity.

Re-authoring conversations

No account of the application of narrative practice in work with people who have been subject to trauma would be sufficient without reference to the part played by what I refer to as the 're-authoring conversations map'. While it is not my intention to fully review this re-authoring conversations map in the space of this chapter, I will provide a flavour of the practices associated with this map here. There are numerous sources available to readers who wish to develop a more intimate familiarity with the therapeutic practices associated with this map (for example: White, 1991, 1995; Morgan 2000; Freedman & Combs 1996).

The re-authoring conversations map features two landscapes, a landscape of action and a landscape of identity[5] (this notion of dual landscapes is borrowed from the work of Jerome Bruner, 1986, and the literary theorists, Griemas and Courtes, 1976) In the diagram below (Diagram 1) these two landscapes are represented by two parallel horizontal time-lines that run through the present, recent history, distant history and near future.

Diagram I

Landscape of Identity _____

| | *Distant History* | | *Recent History* | *Present* | *Near Future* |

Landscape of Action _____

| | *Distant History* | | *Recent History* | *Present* | *Near Future* |

Landscape of action

The landscape of action is composed of events that are linked in sequences, through time, according to a theme or a plot. These four elements seem to represent the rudimentary structure of stories. For example, upon reading a novel one is engaged in an account of specific events that are linked in some sort of sequence, not necessarily lineal, through time and according to a theme or a plot. The plot might be romance, or tragedy, or comedy, or farce, or whatever.

Landscape of identity

The landscape of identity is composed of categories of identity that are like filing cabinets of the mind. These categories of identity are culture specific, and might include motives, attributes, personality traits, strengths, resources, needs, drives, intentions, purposes, aspirations, values, beliefs, hopes, dreams, commitments, etc.

It is into these filing cabinets of the mind that people file a range of identity conclusions. These identity conclusions are usually arrived at through reflection on the events of life that are mapped into landscapes of action. According to the 'constitutive perspective' that shapes narrative practice, people's lives are not shaped by things with names like motives and personality traits, but by the conclusions about one's motives and personality traits that get filed into these filing cabinets of the mind.

In therapeutic conversations that are oriented by the re-authoring conversations map, it is the therapist's task to provide a scaffold through questions that makes it possible for people to draw together, into a storyline, many of the neglected but more sparkling events and actions of their lives. It is also the therapist's task to provide a scaffold that assists people to reflect on the events and the themes of this alternative storyline as it develops, and to derive conclusions about their identities that contradict many of the existing deficit-based identity conclusions that have been so limiting of their lives.

I wish to briefly illustrate the relevance of re-authoring conversations to working with people who have experienced trauma. To do this, I will return to the story of my work with Julie. As I proceed with this illustration you might find it helpful to refer to Diagram II which provides a pictorial account of the zigzagging nature of these re-authoring conversations.

It is possible to review the definitional ceremony practices featured in the story about my work with Julie and to plot these tellings and retellings into the re-authoring conversations map. As readers will recall, one of the experiences that Julie talked about was of her paralysis in response to witnessing a child being run down by a motor car (this is landscape of action material – see #1 on diagram II). In our conversations, it was the story about this event and Julie's response to it that provided an avenue for getting onto what it was that Julie accorded value to in life – she treasured children's lives (this is landscape of identity material – see #2).

Diagram II

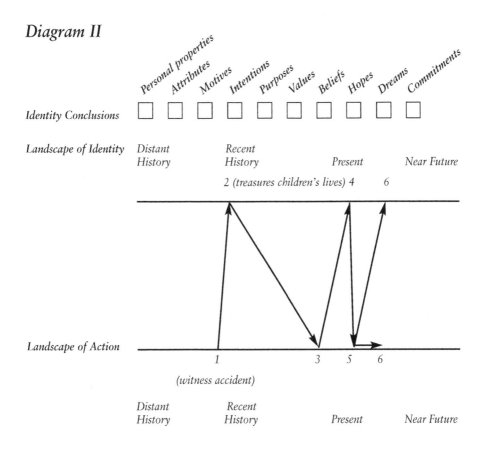

I then arranged a context in which Julie experienced responses that were powerfully resonant with what she accorded value to. This was achieved in the outsider-witness retellings. These outsider witnesses spoke of what they were drawn to in Julie's story (landscape of action material – see #3), about the images of her identity that were evoked by this (landscape of identity material – see #4), about what resonances this set of in their own personal experience (landscape of action material – see #5), and about the ways in which this had moved them (landscape of action and landscape of identity material – see #6).

In the third part of this meeting, I interviewed Julie about what she had heard in the retellings of the outsider witnesses. This interview was informed by the same four categories of inquiry that had shaped these retellings. In response to my questions, Julie spoke about the outsider-witness expressions that had captured her attention (landscape of action material), about the mental pictures of her life that had been evoked by these expressions (landscape of identity material), about what experiences had come to light for her on account of this (landscape of action material), and about how this might affect her perspective on life (landscape of identity material). This could also be charted onto Diagram II.

In my second meeting with Julie, I proceeded to interview her in ways that were shaped by the re-authoring conversations map of narrative therapy. I will now provide a sample of this conversation and plot this onto Diagram III.

Michael: *At the end of our first meeting, I asked you about what you'd heard from the outsider witnesses that had caught your attention, and about what this had set off for you. Amongst other things, you talked about how this had strengthened your realisation about how precious children's lives are to you, and about how this must have always been true for you. I became curious about the sort of stories you might be able to tell me about your life when you were younger that would reflect this high value you give to children's lives?*

This is a landscape of action question about the *events* of Julie's history. This landscape of action question was referenced to a landscape of identity development, which featured a stronger realisation about the value that Julie gives to children's lives.

Diagram III

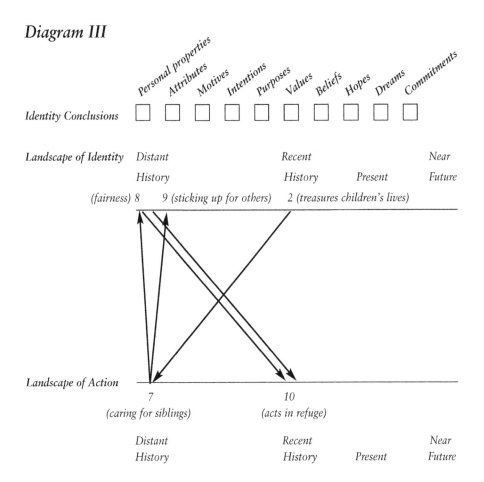

Julie: *Well … er … Right now I can't think of anything to tell you. See, I have lots of problems with my memories. Lots of blank spaces … so I just don't know.*

Julie's response of 'not knowing' suggested that it would be necessary for me to be more active in providing a scaffold for this re-authoring conversation. It was my assumption that in the context of the further scaffolding of this conversation, Julie would find herself to be more knowledgeable in response to this inquiry about her life.

Michael: *I understand that you have a younger brother and a younger sister. If your brother and sister could be here with us today, and they were listening to our conversation, could you guess at the sort of stories they might tell me about you that would reflect the high value that you place on children's lives?*

Julie: *If my brother and sister could be here, what they would say about me?*

Michael: *Yes. If I could ask your sister and your brother to tell me stories about you that would reflect how children's lives are precious to you, what sorts of stories do you think they would they tell me?*

Here I am attempting to evoke the presence of Julie's brother and sister[6]. Asking Julie to represent her brother and sister on matters of her own identity has the potential to provide her with distance from the immediacy of her own experience, and from what is so known and familiar to her (i.e. the many highly negative conclusions about her own identity). I hoped that this distancing manoeuvre, one that encouraged Julie to step into the consciousness of her brother and sister on matters of her own identity, would provide a foundation for Julie to arrive at a different sort of knowing in relation to my question about her younger life.

Julie: 'Okay. Let's see ... I know! I can think of something that my sister might tell you about me when I was just a little girl'

Michael: 'Okay. What story would she tell me?'

Julie: 'She'd tell you a story of when I was a little girl ... maybe I was 9 or 10 years of age at the time. She would tell you that whenever I saw that my father was drinking too much alcohol, and I knew that there was a good chance that he would hurt us, I would gather up my brother and sister and rush them away to a hiding place in the woods near our home. It would be my job to protect them because I was the eldest, and there really was no-one else to turn to. We would wait in this hiding place until I thought it was safe to go back home, when my father was laid out unconscious from drinking too much.

Michael: *That's quite a story!*

Julie: *And I remember ... Yeah, now I remember I used to leave things to eat and drink in this hideaway, and things for my brother and sister to play with, so that they wouldn't be hungry or thirsty, and so that they would be entertained.*

This is landscape of action material (see #7) and isn't it an extraordinary story? It's a beautiful account of some of the actions of Julie's history that reflect what she treasured – the lives of her siblings as children. As therapists we will not hear such stories unless we take great care with the questions that we ask. And the people who consult us will not recall such stories unless we take responsibility for the scaffolding of these re-authoring conversations. I believe that tracing the history of what Julie accorded value to in this way contributed to a dawning, for Julie, of a consciousness of the fact that what she accorded value in the present was part of a theme that stretched through her history: a dawning of some explicit appreciation of a theme that was continuous in her life, one around which many of her actions were linked through time. It was my guess that the dawning of this consciousness would contribute to the redevelopment of that 'sense of myself' that I referred to earlier in this presentation.

Michael: *Julie, imagining that your brother and sister were present, if I asked them what it was these actions of yours told them about you, what's your guess about what they would say? Or if I was to ask them about how this shaped their picture of you as a person, what's your guess about how they might respond? Or if I asked them about what this said to them about what you stood for in life, what do you think they would tell me?*

These are landscape of identity questions. They are not about actions, but they are referenced to new accounts of Julie's actions. These questions invite reflections on actions to derive new conclusions about the person's identity. They invite reflections on actions to determine what these actions suggest about the character of the person, or about the person's purposes, values and beliefs, and so on.

Julie: *Let me think for a bit.. What would this have said to my sister? I guess it would have said something to her about what I stand for in regard to fairness. Yeah. I suppose about my position on injustice.*

Michael: *And your brother?*

Julie: *Well I think it would have told him something about ... let's see ... about, well, perhaps it would have said something to him about my belief in how important it is stick up for people who are going through hard times.*

These words contributed to the development of new identity conclusions (landscape of identity material – see #8 and #9), which are in stark contrast to the negative conclusions that Julie was giving voice to at the beginning of our first meeting. Just imagine these new conclusions being filed into those filing cabinets of the mind that I referred to earlier in this chapter. Just imagine these new conclusions taking up the space that was once occupied by those previously filed negative conclusions.

Michael: *About where you stand on injustice! And about how important it is to stick up for people who are going through hard times!*

Julie: *Yeah. That's it.*

Michael: *Can you think of any more recent events of your life that might be examples of where you stand on injustice, and of your belief in sticking up for people who are going through hard times?*

This is a landscape of action question that is referenced to developments in landscape of identity conclusions. It is a question about any actions/events that might reflect these principles and beliefs that Julie holds dear.

Julie: *Let me think for a bit ... I am not sure that I can come up with anything. I'm sorry, but I can't remember anything like this.*

Michael: *Try casting your mind back over the last few weeks or so. Perhaps over the time that you have been staying at the women's refuge. Anything, anything at all that you can think of in these weeks that could be an example of your position on injustice, or of your belief in sticking up for people who are going through hard times, would be helpful.*

Julie: *Well maybe ... maybe I can think of an example. But I've not thought about this before, so I could be wrong.*

Michael: *What is it?*

Julie: *There's this other woman whose name is Bev. She is staying in the refuge, and she's had a really hard time. I think that she's been terrorised. She doesn't speak, and mostly she splits off from everybody. But I have been sitting with her at lunch times, just being with her. I make it clear to her that I don't expect her to speak, and that I am just there to sit with her* (landscape of action material – see #10). *I think that she knows that I know something about what she has been through, and that this is why she doesn't speak. I think that she knows that what she has been through is not okay with me, but that it is just fine for her not to speak.*

Michael: *Could this be an example of your position on injustice, and about how important it is to you to stick up for people who are going through hard times?*

Julie: *Well, it's like I said. I haven't ever thought about this before. But now I reckon that it could be an example of this. Yeah, it really could.*

This recent expression of solidarity with this other woman in the refuge provided options for further landscape of identity and landscape of action questions, and over the course of the next forty minutes, in the context of this zigzagging re-authoring conversation, the alternative story of Julie's life and identity was more richly developed. It is in actual conversations like these that the reconstruction of identity proceeds. It is in actual conversations like these that a 'sense of myself' is gradually redeveloped and reinvigorated. It is through this redevelopment and reinvigoration that, in the place of a sense of discontinuity, Julie began to experience a continuity of a preferred sense of self through many of the episodes of her history. This was a preferred sense of self that was an expression of what she valued, and of acts of personal agency founded upon what she valued.

The focus of this re-authoring conversation with Julie was on story development. This conversation brought together numerous previously neglected events of Julie's life into a sequence that unfolded through time, according to specific themes. These were themes that contradicted the themes of 'life as tragedy', of 'life as futility'. The development of the alternative storyline is usually gradual and progressive. Returning to some of the metaphors of territory that I proposed earlier in this chapter, we can conceive of these conversations contributing to the gradual opening of neglected territories of life, beginning with atolls, then islands, then archipelagos, and then continents.

To summarise my meetings with Julie: At the outset I listened carefully to her stories of existence in an effort to identify what she accorded value to. Then, through my responses and through the retellings of the outsider witnesses, what Julie accorded value to was re-presented in powerfully resonant ways. I then interviewed Julie about her experience of the retellings of the outsider witnesses, and, amongst other things, this evoked yet other images of her life and identity that were harmonious with these resonant responses. These images then provided the point of entry to an extended re-authoring conversation. This had the effect of regenerating, for Julie, a 'sense of myself' that provided her with an experience of continuity in existence through the episodes of her life. This is an achievement that is of critical importance in work with people who have been subject to trauma.

It's important to note that throughout the therapeutic conversations shaped by the definitional ceremony metaphor and by the re-authoring conversations map, the therapist does not have a role as a primary author of the alternative stories of people's lives. In my work with Julie, the account of what she gave value to represented a thin trace of an alternative story of her life, one that might be richly developed in our conversation. But I could never know any of the particularities of this alternative story ahead of Julie's responses to my landscape of action questions. And, ahead of my landscape of identity questions, I could not assume to know what some of the neglected events of Julie's history might reflect about her identity that would be resonant for her. I was not the author of any of these accounts of her actions or any of these new identity conclusions. However, I was influential by way of the therapeutic structures that I introduced, and by way of the questions that I asked. It is my understanding that these structures and questions provided a scaffold that made it possible for Julie to separate from the known and familiar, and to arrive at new conclusions about her life and her identity.

PART THREE
Memory systems and the consequences of trauma

The consequences of trauma impinge on people's lives in various ways. For many, this is via traumatic memories which invade their lives, and which intrude on their sense of self in a myriad of ways. Because of this, the study of the effects of trauma on people's lives has drawn very significantly on explorations of human memory systems. As considerations of memory are primary in the understanding of the consequences of trauma, and to the development of healing practices, I will now turn to the subject of memory theory. Although most of my understandings about what is relevant to working with people who have been subject to trauma are founded on explorations of narrative practice, I have found memory theory to be highly reinforcing of these understandings. Memory theory has also made it possible for me to fine tune some of my therapeutic practices, and to 'push the envelope' a little in this work.

My knowledge of memory theory, and of the effects of trauma on memory, is drawn principally, though not entirely, from the work of Russell Meares[7]. Much of what I am to share with you about these subjects is drawn from what I learned in participating with Russell Meares in a conference forum a few years ago, and in reading his book *Intimacy and Alienation* (2000) .

Memory systems

As an outcome of explorations of human memory, it is now generally accepted by many memory theorists that there are several distinct memory systems, and that these develop sequentially from birth. Tulving (1993), in drawing together various contributions to the understanding of memory, defined five memory systems that are considered to develop sequentially in the course of human development. These memory systems, in order of development, are: (a) perceptual representation, (b) procedural, (c) semantic, (d) episodic, and (e) short-term memory. I will briefly discuss each of these here, as well as a memory system that Nelson (1992) has referred to as autobiographical, and a memory system that Meares, following William James (1892), refers to as the 'stream of consciousness'.

i) *Perceptual Representation System – 'recognition memory'*
    The perceptual representation system (PRS) is about recognition memory. In the first week after birth, infants begin to recognise a range of familiar stimuli, including voices, actions, shapes and scents. The PRS is a recognition memory in which distinct sensory experience is recorded. In that this recording does not involve explicit recollection of previous experience, this memory system is non-verbal and non-conscious. It is non-conscious as it is a memory system which functions without any awareness, on the infant's behalf, that, in recognising familiar stimuli, s/he is remembering.

ii) *Procedural memory – 'recall memory'*
    Procedural memory is associated with the development of motor skills and repertoires, which are founded on the capacity of the infant to recall experiences of the world. This memory is seen in the capacity of an infant

to bring to mind stimuli that are not immediately present – for example, this memory is present when an infant recalls the existence of toys in a cupboard when the cupboard doors are closed, or when the cupboard is not in the infant's immediate environment – and in the infants capacity to co-ordinate specific motor skills and behavioural repertoires on the basis of this recall. On account of procedural memory, an infant is able to co-ordinate their actions to obtain a particular outcome based on recall (such as to obtain the toys that are in the cupboard). Procedural memory is non-conscious, and, in the first place, non-verbal. It is non-conscious because the child is not aware of the circumstances that gave rise to these learnings.

iii) *Semantic memory*

The second year of life sees the development of what is often called 'semantic memory'. Semantic memory stores what are deemed to be 'facts' – that is, a knowledge of the 'world as it is' – and the child uses this to navigate their way around the world. Semantic memory can be considered a further development of procedural memory. This memory system, which is clearly evident at the end of the second year of life, is verbal – it can be put into words and vocalised.

The development of semantic memory is evident in young children's ability to retain clear memory of the names and attributes of the objects of the world around them, and in their performance of specific routines for going about the world.

This is a memory system that stores a range of learnings about the world which can be vocalised, but which are implicit or non-conscious in the sense that these learnings are recalled without memory of the specific incidents that gave rise to them. The language associated with the semantic memory system is one of coping and adaptation.

iv) *Episodic memory*

Episodic memory develops during the third year of life. By the time children turn three years of age they have the ability to recount experiences of the recent past as specific episodes of their history. These personal memories of the episodic memory system are verbal – they can be vocalised – and are explicit or conscious memories. In the recounting of these recent episodes of personal experience, the child is aware that s/he is remembering specific incidents of his/her life, and does not confuse these with present experience.

v) *Short-term memory – 'working memory'*
The short-term memory system is often referred to as 'working memory'. This is a memory system that stores memories of experiences of the many recent incidents of people's lives, and provides them with immediate orientation in their efforts to achieve specific and complex tasks. A person's capacity to do half a dozen things at once is founded on working memory. Short-term memory is associated with episodic memory, although it is principally a temporary storage system for experiences of the recent incidents of people's lives. This is a verbal and conscious memory system, which is also evident in children's lives by the age of three.

vi) *Auto-biographical memory*
Nelson (1992) distinguishes between these short-lived memories of the recent episodes of one's life that are part of the short-term memory system, and those episodic memories that are highly selected, enduring and often remote. She proposed that these highly selected, enduring and often remote episodic memories provide the foundation for the development of an autobiographical memory that develops in the fifth year of life. It is this autobiographical memory that provides the foundation for a sense of personal identity of the sort that makes it possible for people to assert 'this is my life, and this is me'.

The relatively stable, formal and factual stories that we tell when accounting for our personal history are of auto-biographical memory. Autobiographical memory is both conscious and verbal. This memory system contributes to and is dependent upon the development of a reflexive capacity – a capacity that makes it possible for a person to say: 'This is me', 'Let me tell you about me', 'Let me tell you about my life', and to declare: 'These are my thoughts', 'These are my memories', 'These are my reflections', 'This is my story', 'This is my life'.

vii) Stream of consciousness

There is another memory system that provides for the development of a particular sense of self that is not accounted for by autobiographical memory. It is this memory system that contributes to the development of a continuity of a familiar sense of who one is in the flow of one's inner experiences of life. It is a memory system that accounts for people's capacity to arrange aspects of their lived experiences into the sort of sequences that provides them with a sense of their lives unfolding through time, and with a sense of personal coherence. It is a memory system that makes it possible for people to weave pieces of diverse experience and otherwise disconnected events into coherent themes. It is a memory system that is present to us as a language of inner life.

The stream of consciousness appears narrative in form (James 1892). In the stream of consciousness, many aspects of a person's experiences are organised according to the sort of progressive and associative non-linear sequencing that is a feature of narrative structure. Imagination and pretence feature strongly in this stream, as does analogy, metaphor and simile.

For most of us this stream of consciousness is ever-present as a background to our daily encounter with life, and, at times when we are occupied with the performance of important tasks, it is barely experienced. However, in states of reverie or meditation, when we have stepped back from tasks of living and from our immediate social and relational contexts, we often experience immersion in this stream of consciousness. At such times we become more aware of the roaming and wandering form of this inner language, of the ebbs and flows that characterise it, and of images and themes that are associated with it. And at times we are able to hold these images before us for an extended period of time[8].

I, Me, and Myself

William James proposed that the development of this stream of consciousness is associated with a 'doubling of consciousness' (1892). He drew attention to the fact that when we are remembering we are not just recalling to mind specific episodes of our lives, but we are also conscious of the fact that this is an episode of our own past that we are recalling. We are conscious of the fact that we are reviving what we have experienced in our past, of the fact that we have had this thought or experience before. While remembering, we remain more or less aware of our personal existence – we are not only the 'known', but also the 'knower'.

This is what James referred to as the doubling of consciousness – the emergence of a knower that can be referred to as the 'I', and of the known that can be referred to as the 'me'. It is from the position of 'I' that our attention is directed, from which our diverse experiences of life are unified to form a sense of personal existence, and from where personal reality is constructed.

Meares (2000) suggests that there is more than a doubling of consciousness associated with this phenomenon – he concludes that personal existence is not double, but 'triparate' (in three inter-related parts). He bases this conclusion on the observation that it is possible for one to have experiences in which there exists a sense of 'me', in that one remains certain of one's identity ('Look, I know it is me ...'), but at the same time to be devoid of a familiar sense of 'myself' ('... but, I am just not myself'). That is, there are experiences in which autobiographical memory may be present, providing a person with a sense of me-ness, but in which the language of inner life that is narrative in form and that gives rise to personal reality and a sense of well-being is absent.

In his reading of James, Meares concludes that James was in fact talking about two relatively distinct experiences of the self, founded on two doublings of consciousness, one that provides for the experience of an 'I' in relation to 'me', and the other that provides for an 'I' in relation to 'myself'. According to this formulation, the 'I' in relation to 'me' is relatively invariant, while the 'I' in relation to 'myself' is variable, constantly in flux. This version of 'me' is founded on the sort of factual knowledge that is recorded in autobiographical memory, while this version of 'myself' is relatively plastic, consistently being visioned and re-visioned in response to one's encounters with life, continuously undergoing construction and reconstruction.

Effects of trauma on memory systems

Traumatic memory is invariably triggered by a general stress, by specific circumstances of duress, and/or by specific cues. These cues mirror some aspect of the original trauma, and they may be internal, as in a specific emotional and sensory experience, or external, as in specific circumstances or relational events. These external cues can be associated with circumstances in which there is a perceived absence of social validation, or with experiences of diminishment, perhaps associated with ridicule or criticism.

I will now briefly summarise the principle effects of trauma upon memory systems as described by Meares and by other investigator-theorists.

Dissociation

In our work in the trauma area, it is quite common to meet people who are experiencing the phenomenon of dissociated memories. These are traumatic memories that are not experienced as memories of past experiences, but are located and re-experienced in the present. These traumatic memories intrude on the memory system that is associated with the stream of consciousness, and upon which the sense of myself is founded. When these intrusions are severe, they can totally erase one's familiar sense of personal reality, and contribute to a sense of detachment, desolation, exhaustion, and to an acute sense of vulnerability. These dissociated traumatic memories are usually split off from ordinary consciousness – one is not aware of their origins.

Hierarchical dissolution

It is apparent that those memory systems which evolve later and which develop more slowly are more fragile and more vulnerable to the sort of assault associated with trauma. Jackson (1931) proposed that the more significant the assault the greater the regress in regard to the developmental pathway of memory. According to this proposal, memory systems fail in a hierarchical manner – the later forming and more sophisticated memory systems fail first. Moderate trauma can have the effect of inactivating the stream of consciousness, contributing to a loss of the sense of 'myself'. With the dissolution of the stream of consciousness, people will feel a loss of substance, an emptiness, a sense of personal weightlessness and desolation.

Moderate and recurring trauma can have the effect of erasing not just the flow of consciousness, but also the autobiographical and episodic memory systems. With the loss of autobiographical memory, people will experience difficulty in putting together an account of the trajectory of their life through time, and the sense of 'this is me' will become quite elusive. When short-term memory is affected, it becomes very difficult to cope with more than one task at a time, and people will report feeling chronically stressed over the simple tasks of daily life.

This theory of hierarchical dissolution also proposes that the more recurring the trauma the more likely it is to be stored in non-conscious memory systems. For example, experiences of more severe and recurring trauma may be stored in the semantic memory, or in procedural memory and in the perceptual representation system. According to this theory, more severe trauma can contribute to the failing of semantic memory as well, so that only procedural memory and perceptual representation systems are operative.

Uncoupling

When traumatic memories intrude into everyday consciousness, very often the outcome is an uncoupling of consciousness – the doubling of consciousness is dissolved. One no longer has a vantage point in which to stand in the present that makes possible an awareness that what one is experiencing is from another time in one's life.

This uncoupling of consciousness contributes to a dismantling of a familiar sense of self that has continuity across time – the experience of an 'I' in relation to 'myself', and at times the experience of 'I' in relation to 'me' is significantly reduced, and on occasions lost. The capacity to evaluate and monitor one's experiences and actions is then very significantly reduced, and can be entirely erased when these intrusive memories are of severe and recurrent trauma.

Meaning

Even in the midst of traumatic experience, people endeavour to make sense of what is happening to them. For many, although not all, the experience of trauma is irreconcilable with any familiar themes and with any preferred account of one's identity. These are themes and accounts of identity that are associated with autobiographical memory and with a language of inner life that organises experience and that has a structure that is characteristic of narrative.

The irreconcilable nature of traumatic experience takes one into territories of meaning that are split off from these familiar themes and narrative of self. On account of this, the meanings that are manufactured in these territories are usually profoundly negative, and not open to revision in the way that those associated with the narrative of self are open to revision – other experiences of one's life that might contradict these meanings have little effect on them. These other experiences do not contribute to a revision of these meanings. These meanings that are manufactured in the context of trauma become virtually unassailable facts about one's identity[9].

Devaluation

The experience of recurrent trauma can contribute to the establishment of highly negative conclusions about one's identity and life that achieve the status of invariant facts. Trauma also contributes to a diminishment of what it is that a person attributes value to, of what is held precious, of what is essential to one's sense of personal integrity; that is, to the devaluation of the images, memories, conclusions and sentiments about life and identity that provide people with a sense of personal intimacy and from which they draw a sense of personal warmth and positive feelings.

It is the devaluation of what is given value and held precious that leads very significantly to the development of a sense of being 'damaged', 'messed up', and 'disabled'.

Chronicle

When the stream of consciousness is impinged upon by traumatic memories, life is experienced as just one thing after another, and is invariably recounted to others as a problem-saturated and fragmentary catalogue of events. This is a recounting of life that lacks vitality and animation – it is flat, dead. The language employed in this recounting is linear and matter-of-fact, and it contains no evidence of any content of an inner personal reality – it is devoid of metaphor, association, and co-ordinating themes that provide for a sense of existence that is ongoing and unfolding; it is devoid of a sense of unity and continuity of self.

With this breakdown of the sense of continuity of existence and personal cohesion, one becomes captive to the present moment, trapped by particular stimuli. Gone is the option to roam about in time. Gone too is the option of playing a co-ordinating and synthesising role in one's own life; of self regulation, and of the sense of personal agency that is associated with this.

I will now turn to discussion of some of the therapeutic implications of these understandings of the effects of trauma on memory systems. Although I have often employed other terms to describe my work with people who have been subject to trauma, I share Russell Meares sentiments about the primary therapeutic task: that is the reinvigoration and redevelopment of the memory system called the stream of consciousness in the instatement/reinstatement of a 'sense of myself'. I also share Russell Meares' sentiments about the route to achieving this: that is, through the identification of what it is that people accord value to, and by establishing responses that are resonant with this. In the translation of these sentiments into practice there are divergences in regard to our respective positions – my translations are very much the outcome of a tradition of narrative explorations of therapeutic practice.

Therapeutic implications

It is invariably the case that efforts to directly address people's experiences of trauma by encouraging them to revisit this are unproductive at best, and, in many circumstances, hazardous. Such efforts can contribute to experiences of re-traumatisation, and to a renewed sense of alienation. And to engage in efforts to directly contradict and to destabilise the negative conclusions about a person's identity that are generated in the context of trauma, conclusions that might be stored in the semantic memory system and that have the status of fact, can be experienced as disrespectful and patronising, and even mocking.

The primary therapeutic task in addressing the effects of trauma on people's lives is to provide a context for the development or redevelopment of the sort of personal reality that gives rise to the sense of self that is often referred to as 'myself'. This is the sense of self that is associated with the development of a language of inner life that is narrative in form and that characterises what William James called the 'stream of consciousness'.

From a narrative perspective, the development or redevelopment of this sense of an inner life can be achieved, in part, through a therapeutic inquiry that provides a scaffold for people to bring together diverse experiences of life into a storyline that is unifying of these experiences, and that provides for them a sense of personal continuity through the course of their history. The arrangement of experiences of life around specific themes and relevant metaphors contributes significantly to this unification and sense of continuity, and to the reinstatement of the doubling of consciousness referred to in this presentation as the 'I' in relation to 'myself'.

Re-valuation and resonance

In the examples that I have given in this chapter, therapeutic inquiry has first been directed to the identification of those aspects of life to which people have accorded value. This might be: specific purposes for one's life that are cherished; prized values and beliefs with regard to acceptance, justice and fairness; treasured aspirations, hopes and dreams; personal pledges, vows and commitments to ways of being in life; special memories, images, and fantasies about life that are linked to significant themes; metaphors that represent special realms of existence; and so on. In the context of the therapeutic conversations I have described, these aspects of people's lives were identified and re-valued through a range of resonant responses.

It is not always easy to identify those aspects of life to which people have accorded value – they have often been secreted away in places where they are safe from further ridicule and diminishment – and even when identified, it can be quite a task for people to name them. However, despite any initial difficulties in identifying those aspects of life to which people accord value, I believe that these are ever-present in people's expressions of life. I believe this to be so even when these people are regularly experiencing life through the thrall of dissociated traumatic memories – as Meares (2000) observes, even at this time there is some principle operating in the selection of memories. This fact is an extraordinary tribute to the person's refusal to relinquish or to be separated from what was so powerfully disrespected and demeaned in the context of trauma.

Once identified, whatever it is about life and identity to which the person has accorded value provides an orientation for the development of resonance within the therapeutic conversation. In this presentation I have presented examples of therapeutic practices that contribute a scaffold to develop this resonance. One of these examples was the story about my work with Julie who, over a number of meetings, and on occasions with the active participation of the refuge workers and other women living in the refuge, was able to redevelop a rich 'sense of myself', and, as an outcome of this, never returned to live with the man who had been abusive of her.

Re-associating dissociated memory

Because dissociated memories stand outside of and are independent of people's lives, they are timeless memories; these memories are apart from the storylines of people's lives which are constituted of experiences linked in sequences across time according to specific themes. Being located on the outside of the dimension of time, these traumatic memories have no beginning and no end. When traumatic memories are beyond time in this way, there is always the potential for particular circumstances to trigger the re-living of these memories in real time. These traumatic memories are re-lived as present experience and the outcome is re-traumatisation.

Apart from being timeless memories, dissociated memories are half memories. What is excluded from dissociated memory is an account of the person's response to what they were being subject to. People are not passive recipients of the traumas they are subject to. Even if they are powerless to significantly influence what they are being put through, or have no options for escaping the traumatic context, they take what steps are available to them to modify what they are being subject to in some small way, or to modify the effects of this trauma on their lives and identities. Not only are the details of these responses excluded from dissociated memory, but the foundations of these responses are also erased; that is, what it was that the person continued to accord value to through this experience, including their sentiment of living, and the practices of life associated with this sentiment of living. Put in other words, traumatic memories are half memories as they exclude an account of personal agency that would be in harmony with the persons' familiar and preferred sense of myself.

There are many factors that contribute to the development of dissociated memory. These include the fact that the experience of trauma is:

a) irreconcilable with what people accord value to;

b) in many cases a direct assault on what people hold precious;

c) irreconcilable with many of the culture's cherished notions of life;

d) often associated with the active diminishment, disqualification, and punishment of people's responses to what they are being put through, and what it is that provides the foundations of these responses.

In order to re-associate dissociated memories, it is necessary to restore these half memories to full memories. In other words, the task is to resurrect that which is erased in dissociated memory – that is, people's responses to what they were being put through, and the foundations of these responses. This resurrection is restorative of a sense of personal agency, one that is in harmony with the person's preferred 'sense of myself'. This is the 'sense of myself' that I have referred to on many occasions in the course of this chapter, one that provides an experience of continuity of personhood through the many episodes of one's history. The restoration of these memories to full memories provides the foundation for them to be taken into history in the storylines of people's lives – in being restored in these ways, these memories carry with them accounts of personhood that are no longer alien, and this provides conditions for these memories to be taken into the storylines of people's lives in ways that provides them with beginnings and endings in time. When traumatic memory is re-associated in this way, the potential for these memories to be re-traumatising is very significantly diminished.

These considerations relating to the re-association of dissociated memory further emphasise the importance of the priority given in this work to the reinvigoration and redevelopment of the 'sense of myself'. Dissociated memory cannot be re-associated if there is no receiving frame to take this into; if there is no storyline through which can be traced a preferred 'sense of myself' through the many episodes of personal history. Once there is progress in the reinvigoration and redevelopment of this 'sense of myself', people can be assisted to imaginatively speculate about how they may have responded to the traumas of their history, and about the foundation of these responses. In this imaginative speculation, people are encouraged to project back, into the history of their lives, what is becoming more richly known about their sentiment of life, and about the practices of living that are associated with this, including their practices of counter-power.

I would add here that, in my experience, this imaginative speculation is not always necessary in the re-association of dissociated memory. In many instances the reinvigoration and redevelopment of this 'sense of myself' in the way that I have described in this chapter provides conditions for the spontaneous re-association of dissociated memory; in the course of these therapeutic conversations, experiences of trauma often come into conscious memory and are allocated to history for the first time.

Returning to the story of Julie, once she'd had the opportunity to richly develop a personal narrative that featured a valued sense of personhood that could be traced through the history of significant events of her life, we were in a position to engage in the imaginative speculation about how she had responded to the trauma she had been subject to as a young girl. This was trauma that she mostly had no conscious recollection of, but sensed she had experienced. This sense was confirmed by information that she'd been given by her brother, sister and a maternal aunt.

This imaginative speculation was based on the many understandings about Julie's sentiment of living, and on the practices of living associated with this, that were generated in the context of our therapeutic conversations (i.e. her position on injustice, her belief in fairness, her commitment to stick up for people who are going through hard times, and the ways in which she treasures children's lives). It was in the context of this speculation that Julie began to recall aspects of her experiences of trauma. Whilst some distress was associated with this recall, this was not re-traumatising of Julie. As an outcome of these efforts to re-associate dissociated memory, she reported a very significant diminution in episodes of profoundly demoralising ideas about her identity, and of the frightening visual images that were often associated with these that just seemed to come out of nowhere.

This is the sort of re-association of dissociated memories that becomes possible when the 'sense of myself' is restored.

Conclusion

This chapter emphasised the priority given to the redevelopment and reinvigoration of a 'sense of myself' in work with people who have been subject to trauma. The contribution of narrative practices associated with definitional ceremony structures, outsider-witness practices and re-authoring conversations to this redevelopment and reinvigoration of a sense of myself were described.

The last section of this chapter focussed on memory theory and its relevance to work with people who have experienced trauma. This memory theory reinforces the importance of the revitalisation of a 'sense of myself'. Amongst other things, this revitalisation is essential in establishing a context for a re-association of dissociated memory.

Notes

1. This sense of myself is a phenomenon of the language of inner life that William James (1892) named the 'stream of consciousness'.

2. Apart from other things, at this time I often find opportunity to assist people to name, often for the first time, the nature of the trauma that they have been put through, and to identity the strategies of power they have been subject to in the context of this trauma. I have discussed this aspect of a narrative approach to addressing trauma elsewhere (White, 1995), and will not focus on this here.

3. At the end of our meetings, Julie insisted that I insert her name and contact details into one of my outsider-witness registers.

4. In according due significance to this achievement, it is helpful for therapists to conceive of the development of these practices of counter-power as a contribution to a wider technology of counter-power.

5. Drawing on literary theory, Bruner (1986) employs the term landscape of consciousness, not identity. I see this as a more adequate description, but it tends to be confusing in the context of the culture of psychotherapy where the term 'consciousness' has different historical associations.

6. Unfortunately, Julie's brother and sister were not available to attend our meetings. Had they been available, I could have invited them to assume the outsider-witness position for some of my conversation with Julie.

7. Russell Meares is a Sydney psychiatrist who has specialised in working with people who have been subject to trauma. I had the good fortune to share a forum with Russell Meares in a psychiatric congress a few years ago, and discovered that we have many shared interests. Not only do we both devote considerable time and thought to the development of approaches to working with trauma, but we also have a common interest in the writings of many interesting thinkers, including William James (1892), Lev Vygotsky (1962), and Gaston Bachelard (1969). As well as this, we have a shared appreciation of the significance of key concepts in the shaping of healing practices, including the concept of 'resonance', and a shared appreciation of the importance of identifying what people 'give value to', which I have referred to many times in this chapter.

8. As the redevelopment and reinvigoration of this stream of consciousness is given priority in work with people who have been subject to trauma, in this endnote I will provide an extended account of this memory system, and of it's development. Much of this account is drawn from the work of William James (1892), Lev Vygotsky (1962), and Gaston Bachelard (1969).

Stream of Consciousness

This is a memory system that provides for the development of a particular sense of self that is not accounted for by autobiographical memory. It is this memory system that contributes to the development of a continuity of a familiar sense of who one is in the flow of one's inner experiences of life.

This familiar sense of who one is in the flow of inner experience is the outcome of social collaboration. It arises through the internalisation of a special conversation that is significantly present in children's lives from around eighteen months of age. This is a conversation that features speech that is non-linear and associative, and that is not apparently in the service of any outward purpose – it is not of the speech that is characteristic in a child's efforts to relate to the objects of his/her world. This special conversation is often defined as egocentric speech because its purpose does not appear to be communicative – rather, it is associated with the development of symbolic play, and of play with symbols.

This symbolic play and this play with symbols is a social or relational achievement. As part of this achievement, caretakers engage in a range of activities that provide a 'scaffold' that makes it possible for the child to distance from the immediacy of their experience. For example, caretakers routinely mirror or imitate the infant's expressions and actions in ways that contribute to the child's recognition of a 'me' – this is a me that arises from a re-presentation of the child's expressions and actions. Caretakers also introduce the young child to the sort of pretence and mimicry that encourages the child to imitate others, and that provides a foundation for the development of symbolic play which often features illusionary people, and through which an outside and alien world is rendered personal and familiar. Further, in the context of rudimentary games, caretakers introduce young children to practices of turn-taking and sequencing which are essential to the development of conversational ability. This is also essential to building the child's capacity to arrange aspects of their lived experiences into the sort of sequences that provides them with a sense of their lives unfolding through time, and with a sense of personal coherence. As well, these rudimentary games introduce to children a culture of problem solving.

These special conversations that are associated with symbolic play, and in which the child constructs a personal reality that gives rise to a sense of self, appear to be organised according to the structure of narrative. In the production of these conversations, caretakers build contexts that facilitate children's meaning-making. In these conversations, young children are provided with structure and with frames of meaning-making that make it possible for them to weave pieces of diverse experience and otherwise disconnected events into coherent themes. In this weaving, the child has the opportunity to organise many aspects of their experience according to the sort of progressive and associative non-linear sequencing that is a feature of narrative structure. Imagination and pretence feature strongly in these conversations, as does the development of analogy, metaphor and simile. In this special conversation, objects of the world that are alien are transformed into phenomena of a familiar world that is sensed as 'my world', into a world that is 'mine', as distinct from a world that is not.

In the fourth year of life this egocentric speech becomes increasingly broken, abbreviated, and condensed as it is progressively internalised (as Vygotsky proposes). It then begins to disappear. It is through the internalisation of this symbolic play, which is mostly achieved by around the age of five years, that the child develops an inner reality. This becomes the language of inner life, and is what William James referred to as the 'stream of consciousness'. For most of us this stream of consciousness is ever-present as a background to our daily encounter with life. It is in states of reverie, in which we have stepped back from tasks of living and from our immediate social and relational contexts, that we experience immersion in this stream of consciousness. At such times we become aware of the roaming and wandering form of this inner language, of the ebbs and flows that characterise it, and of images and themes that are associated with it.

At these times we also experience the phenomena of reverberation and resonance – the images and themes associated with this inner language have the potential to set off reverberations that reach into the history of our lived experience, and, in response to these reverberations, we experience the resonance of specific memories of our past. These memories light up, are often powerfully visualised, and are taken into the personal storylines of our lives, resulting in a heightened sense of myself. All of this is experienced while at the same time one is aware that it is 'I' who is doing the remembering.

It is the development of this personal reality through the internalisation of this language of inner life that provides us with a sense of personal intimacy. It is also this development that provides a foundation for achieving a sense of personal intimacy with others. This is an intimacy that depends upon one's ability to express an inner experience that can be shared with others, and that will have a resonance with the inner experience of others. This contributes to a sense of interpersonal familiarity and to a sense of mutual understanding that is the hallmark of relating intimately to others. On this account, the sense of myself, that has its origins in social collaboration, continues to be very significantly a relational phenomenon – to 'feel myself' is very significantly an experience of resonant movements in our intimate relationships.

The internalisation of this language of inner life also makes possible an 'empathic' relationship with aspects of a familiar and understandable world, that would otherwise be alien and inchoate. This is the outcome of experiencing a resonance between the orienting themes, purposes and plans of one's inner life with the unfolding events of external reality – a continuity between inner experience and the outside world.

9. According to some versions of memory theory, these conclusions about identity that are assigned a factual status are stored in semantic memory, and are relatively invulnerable to direct efforts to modify or to disprove them. I have consistently found developments of externalising conversations to be corrosive of these negative conclusions (for example, see White 2001). These externalising conversations have the objective of unpacking these conclusions, and do not constitute efforts to disprove or to modify them.

References

Bachelard, G. 1969: *The Poetics of Space.* Boston: Beacon Press.

Bruner, J. 1986: *Actual Minds, Possible Worlds.* Cambridge, MA: Harvard University Press.

Freedman, J. & Combs, G. 1996: *Narrative Therapy: The social construction of preferred realties.* New York: W. W. Norton & Co.

Griemas, A. & Courtes, J. 1976. *'The cognitive dimension of narrative discourse.' New Literary History.* vol 7, Spring: 433-447

Jackson, H. 1931: *Selected Writings of John Hughlings Jackson, Vol 1 & 2.* J Taylor (Ed), London: Hodder.

James, W. 1892 : *Psychology: Briefer course.* London: Macmillan.

Meares, R. 2000: *Intimacy and Alienation: Memory, trauma and personal being.* London: Routledge.

Morgan, A. 2000: *What is Narrative Therapy? An easy-to-read introduction.* Adelaide: Dulwich Centre Publications.

Myerhoff, B. 1982: 'Life history among the elderly: Performance, visibility and re-membering.' In J Ruby (ed), *A Crack in the Mirror: Reflexive perspectives in anthropology.* Philadelphia: University of Philadelphia Press.

Myerhoff, B. 1986: 'Life not death in Venice: Its second life.' In Turner, V. & Bruner, E. (eds): *The Anthropology of Experience.* Chicago: University of Illinois Press.

Nelson, K. 1992: 'Emergence of autobiographical memory at four.' *Human Development,* 35:172-177.

Russell, S. & Carey, M. 2003: 'Outsider-witness practices: Some answers to commonly asked questions.' *International Journal of Narrative Therapy and Community Work,* No.1.

Tulving, E. 1993: 'What is episodic memory?' *Current Directions in Psychological Science,* 2:67-70.

Vygotsky, L. S. 1962: *Thought and Language.* Cambridge, MA: MIT Press.

White, M. 1991: 'Deconstruction and therapy.' *Dulwich Centre Newsletter,* No.3. Reprinted in Gilligan, S. (ed) 1991: *Therapeutic Conversations.* New York: W. W. Norton.

White, M. 1995a: 'Reflecting teamwork as definitional ceremony.' In White, M.: *Re-Authoring Lives: Interviews and essays.* Adelaide: Dulwich Centre Publications.

White, M. 1995b: 'The narrative perspective in therapy.' In White, M.: *Re-Authoring Lives: Interviews and essays.* Adelaide: Dulwich Centre Publications.

White, M. 1997: *Narratives of Therapists' Lives.* Adelaide: Dulwich Centre Publications.

White, M. 2000a: 'Reflecting-team work as definitional ceremony revisited.' In White, M.: *Reflections on Narrative Practice: Essays and interviews.* Adelaide: Dulwich Centre Publications.

White, M. 2000b: 'Re-engaging with history: The absent but implicit.' In White, M.: *Reflections on Narrative Practice: Essays and interviews.* Adelaide: Dulwich Centre Publications.

White, M. 2001: 'Narrative practice and unpacking identity conclusions.' *Gecko: A journal of deconstruction and narrative practice,* No.1. Reprinted in Zeig, J. (ed) 2003: *The Evolution of Psychotherapy: A meeting of the minds.* Arizona: Milton Erickson Foundation Press.

White, M. 2003: 'Community assignments and narrative practice.' *International Journal of Narrative Therapy and Community Work,* No.2.

CHAPTER THREE

Avoiding psychological colonisation: Stories from Sri Lanka

- responding to the tsunami

by Shanti Arulampalam, Lara Perera,
Sathis de Mel, Cheryl White
& David Denborough

Understandings about trauma and trauma work that have been developed in western countries are now being 'exported' across cultures. What are the implications of this, and how can care be taken not to replicate forms of psychological colonisation? This chapter consists of a series of extracts from interviews from Sri Lankan community workers and psycho-social workers who were involved in responding to the aftermath of the tsunamis of December 2004. These workers are determined to hold onto and utilise local knowledge and expertise in responding to the experience of Sri Lankan communities.

Responding in Sri Lankan ways
Shanti Arulampalam

Shanti Arulampalam is the founder and director of Survivors Associated, an agency that was formed to respond to communities affected by the Sri Lankan civil war. As Shanti describes, despite the magnitude of the disaster, the Sri Lankan people are rebounding.

The tsunami was a major crisis for this country. The loss of life has been enormous and people have been responding in many ways. Obviously there is a lot of work going into rebuilding houses, infrastructure and ways to enable people to get on with their lives. There has also been a lot of thought about ways of assisting people to deal with the shock, the loss and the grief that has been experienced. A psychological approach is only one way of responding to this and it is only appropriate in Sri Lanka when taken together with other responses. In this country, we have many traditions and rich cultural practices which have served us well over thousands of years. We are a very proud people. Our culture spans two thousand years. We have what might be called 'psychosocial strategies' built into our traditions. When a person dies, or when a calamity occurs, there are certain cultural and religious practices that we undertake. There are certain duties and responsibilities that we have to fulfil. These are very appropriate responses for us in difficult situations. After the tsunami, it is to these cultural practices that people first turn. In our work, we are trying to support communities in their own ways of dealing with the effects of the tsunami. Of course, we have also learned from other countries and other traditions, including western traditions, and we combine these interventions with our cultural traditions. When an event of this magnitude occurs we try to build upon what we already know and have used successfully.

As Sri Lankans, we know quite a bit about trauma and dealing with it. If we didn't we'd be in a lot of trouble because we've been dealing with twenty years of armed conflict!

We started our work in communities many years ago with single women whose husbands had been killed or disappeared. Widows in Sri Lanka are often looked down upon. This is one cultural tradition that is not so helpful. In many communities widows are seen as bad luck. They are not encouraged to dress well or take part in community activities and, if they move about in public on their own, they are seen as 'questionable women'. Hardly surprisingly, this can lead to feelings of unworthiness. We brought these women together and created support groups in which they could speak about their experiences and learn from each other. Realising that economic issues were a key issue for these women who were trying to raise their children, the group were given a loan together to start small businesses. Over time these businesses flourished. They even came to own a mill and several small shops. These women who were traditionally shunned had built themselves up into community leaders. And then the tsunami struck. Their homes were washed away. Their property was destroyed. Their businesses were ruined. Some of them lost their children. Several members of the support group themselves were washed away.

I was out of the country when the tsunami occurred and I could not imagine how I was going to face these women after all they had been through. When you work together for a long time, you build up close relationships. What was I going to say to them? How was I going to be able to explain this terrible event, why it has happened to them after all they had been through? I came back to Sri Lanka four days after it had happened and when we met up they were devastated. We cried together. All their efforts had been destroyed. But two weeks later, I went back again and there was such a change. These same women had gathered other women for whom tragedy had struck for the first time. They had formed themselves into a support group. These women were now telling the other women: 'We can't stay down all the time. Nothing will happen unless we do it for ourselves. We need to get up and start doing things'. They had befriended these other women. They were offering support to them. They were saying: 'We were in bad situations before and we got out of it, this is how we did it. We must do it again now.'

One of the women came up to me and said: 'The food in the camps is terrible. If we had the equipment we could cook for the camp, we could sell food for a very cheap price.' And so, we supplied the equipment. This woman had lost everything, but she was quickly responding to this crisis and was getting re-established again. Within two weeks of the tsunamis I had business plans from women's groups on my table. They knew how small sums of grant money could seed community recovery. When I went back to the camps last week I saw a whole range of small businesses in the camps: little grocery shops, people making things, different food stalls.

While there are still many difficulties to address, the strength of these Sri Lankan women is leading a recovery in their villages.

Principles informing responses to communities affected by the tsunami
Lara Perera

Lara Perera is the Psychosocial Coordinator at the Consortium of Humanitarian Agencies in Colombo. The Psycho Social Forum, which Lara facilitates, was originally established in relation to the civil war. It is now playing a key role in co-ordinating responses to the tsunami and enhancing the quality, competence and accountability of psychosocial services in Sri Lanka.

As soon as the Psycho Social Forum came to learn of the extent of the tsunami we began working on a set of principles to guide the ways in which organisations could respond to local communities. These were developed particularly to assist those organisations from outside Sri Lanka that had arrived from overseas and local agencies who had not previously been involved in psychosocial work. We wished to try to ensure these agencies worked as effectively and culturally appropriately as possible and that they 'did no harm' in the process. We developed ten key principles:

1. *To avoid medicalising people's responses*
   Immediately after the tsunami we knew that people in affected areas might be experiencing many different emotional and physical responses. Every individual reacts differently: many people will display amazing strengths and resilience to different degrees in different phases of recovery. At other moments, some will display responses that include confusion, fear, hopelessness, sleeplessness, crying, and difficulty in eating, headaches, body aches, anxiety, and anger. They may be feeling nothing at all or helpless;

some may be in a state of shock; others may be aggressive, mistrustful, feeling betrayed, despairing, feeling relieved or guilty that they are alive, sad that many others have died, and ashamed of how they might have reacted or behaved during the critical incidents. There may be some experiencing a sense of outrage, shaken religious faith, loss of confidence in themselves or others, or sense of having betrayed or been betrayed by others they trusted. These are all normal reactions to extremely dangerous or stressful situations, or where people have felt helpless or overwhelmed. They do not mean that these people are traumatised, mentally disturbed or mentally ill. We have tried to encourage organisations who are working in Sri Lanka not to interpret or diagnose people's immediate reactions to the tsunami as indicating some medical condition (such as PTSD). These are simply normal reactions to a terrible situation.

2. *To question the assumption that Sri Lankans as a group were 'traumatised'*
   Similarly, we do not believe it is helpful for agencies to make assumptions that large numbers of Sri Lankans will be traumatised by this event over the longer term. Sri Lankans know quite a lot about trauma. We have been enduring a situation of war over the last twenty years. We have worked from a different assumption that, providing we can meet basic support services, the vast majority of the people will find ways to support themselves and each other through these times and will not have lasting traumatised responses. Only a small percentage will need specialised care and an even smaller percentage will require mental health services. We have found that one group has been in need of specialised care: this is the group of people who, prior to the tsunami, were already linked with mental health services or mental health support. After the tsunami these people were very vulnerable as they may have lost access to their usual supports and also to their medication. But we feel that the majority of people will come through this very well.

3. *To return to normalcy*
   We have worked from the assumption that the best, most supportive and effective responses from organisations are those that promote and assist a

return to normalcy for community members. For instance, we have needed to question programs that remove children from their usual school routines. We have encouraged agencies to consider how their work can best assist people to get their lives back to their usual routines and practices.

4. *To build upon local resources and knowledge*
   We have encouraged agencies to acknowledge the wealth of existing resources in Sri Lanka in relation to responding to communities in crisis. We suggest agencies use local resources and consult Sri Lankans about local knowledge that is relevant to relating to communities. We've also advised that outside agencies work through existing systems (e.g. the Ministry of Health, or existing organisations) so these local systems are strengthened, rather than weakened, by the influence of outside aid. This has become a significant issue. As large international agencies have arrived with considerable funding, a number of small local agencies have been closed down. We are doing what we can to respond to this and to prevent further occurrences.

5. *To be culturally sensitive*
   We have appealed to international organisations to consider the cultural meaning and implications of all responses and organisational practices. This includes taking into account the religious beliefs of the community. Religion and spiritual beliefs are often an integral aspect of the wellbeing of local people. How locals understand their experiences are powerfully influenced by cultural and religious meanings.

6. *To prioritise community participation and community empowerment*
   It is vital for community members to be involved in service provision in order to avoid dependency. For instance, we learned that in some camps the food supplies were being cooked by aid workers, rather than by local people. This meant that the mothers were displaced from their regular roles of cooking for their families. We also heard about foreign workers doing the labour to build walls and physical structures in villages when these are skills and abilities that local villagers have always done. Involving the community and mobilising their skills and abilities is critical.

7. *To be inclusive of all members of the community*
   We have also tried to encourage community responses that are inclusive of all members of the community. Often particular agencies wish to work only with children, or only with women. Very few organisations provide services for men. We try to raise awareness that responses to communities need to include all community members.

8. *To consider long-term sustainability*
   We are aware that many of the international organisations will only be here for a limited amount of time. We are trying to ensure that the longer-term sustainability of projects is considered.

9. *To consider the ethics and real effects of research projects*
   It seemed that, for some, the tsunami was an opportunity to conduct research on people's reactions. Many people from other countries came to Sri Lanka to do research on people's reactions and much of this research was not being done in culturally appropriate ways. We are not opposed to research, but it has to be done in an ethical and appropriate way. An ethics committee is being established by the Sri Lankan Ministry of Health to oversee all requests.

10. *To share resources and information*
    One of the key aims of our organisation involves networking and co-ordination. We seek to reduce the duplication and to encourage organisations to share resources, ideas and knowledge. We particularly try to encourage agencies to share 'needs assessments' because otherwise some communities are 'assessed' many times over and we are concerned about the effects of this. We are also interested in how these 'assessments' can take place in ways that empower communities. We have heard reports of local people saying: 'The big organisation from overseas came and they told us what we need'! We are interested in alternative processes that genuinely consult communities in ways that are empowering.

As agencies continue to provide much needed food, housing and other forms of practical support, we hope these principles will assist their work with Sri Lankan communities. There are continual challenges, and no doubt we will be generating further principles as time goes on, but these ten principles are providing a framework for constructive conversations and the building of greater teamwork as we work with local communities to rebuild infrastructure, support those most affected, and return to normalcy.

Four alternative approaches to conventional 'needs assessments'

As Lara Perera describes above, there is considerable interest in developing ways of 'assessing' communities which have been affected by disaster that lead to a sense of community empowerment rather than a feeling of hopelessness and dependency. We have included here short excerpts from four alternative approaches to assessment.

Assessing communities' strengths, skills and abilities: An appreciative Inquiry
by Sathis de Mel (from an interview) Arthacharya Foundation, Mount Lavinia, Sri Lanka

Over time we have become concerned with the degree to which conventional 'needs assessments' of communities are problem orientated. We have noticed that only assessing a community's needs can be burdening of local people. Asking questions only about what is lacking in a village can have the effects of being very tough on the poor. We have witnessed that when we are working with the poor of the poor, if we talk only about their problems they become all the more frustrated – with life and with us!

Five years ago I was introduced to the idea of appreciative inquiry (Elliott 1999, Hammond 1998) by Myrada, a community development organisation in Bangalore in South India (see www.myrada.org). We received training in this approach and have subsequently introduced it to some local community organisations. Generally speaking we are encouraged by this orientation. It is clear that people like to talk about their success stories, about their community's strengths and skills. It creates a very different atmosphere.

The aim of our organisation is social mobilisation and we have noticed that, if people are able to acknowledge and take pride in what they have been doing, then this can make a significant contribution towards mobilising future action. It can be a catalyst for people to work together to address current challenges. I believe we can use this approach in communities affected by the tsunami, to remind people of their strengths. As we move out of the immediate recovery and relief phase we are now beginning to look at longer-term approaches, and I believe appreciative inquiry will have a role to play.

Capacities and Vulnerabilities Analysis
Mary B. Anderson

In her book, Rising From the Ashes: Development Strategies in Times of Disaster (Boulder: Westview Press, 1989), Mary Anderson describes a particular framework for assessment in times of disaster. This framework involves exploring a community's needs, vulnerabilities and capacities:

"Needs, as used in a disaster context, refer to immediate requirements for survival or recovery from a calamity ... [they] arise out of the crisis itself, and are relatively short-term ... Vulnerabilities refer to the long-term factors which affect the ability of a community to respond to events or which make it susceptible to calamities ... Vulnerabilities precede disasters, contribute to their severity, impede effective disaster response and continue afterwards ... To avoid increasing vulnerabilities, it is necessary to identify capacities in order to know what strengths exist within a society — even among disaster victims — on which future development can be built." (Anderson 1989, p.10-11)

Building on the skills of community members
America Bracho

The work of Latino Health Access in California has provided an alternative method of responding to communities struggling with the effects of poverty and ill-health. This is an approach that deliberately builds upon the skills of communities rather than focusing upon their needs.

"We work from the belief that every person and every community has skills and knowledges, strengths and assets which when mobolised can contribute to the creation of healthy communities. We do not start by recognising the needs of a community and trying to address these needs. Instead we start by recognising the talents, knowledges and skills of the community. Harnessing these, we believe, is the secret to transforming communities ...

It is our responsibility to provide mechanisms in a sensitive way that enable people to demonstrate, to perform their caring. It is our responsibility to notice and enquire about the assets, talents and skills of the community and to provide contexts by which the people we are working with can take actions to contribute towards the accomplishment of their hopes, aims and dreams. In this process we are creating territories of common ground. The first commonality being that everyone cares about similar issues, the second being that they all have something to contribute in relation to that which they care about. This orientation brings particular responsibilities for workers. We do not believe that 'cultural competence' (which is often talked about in the US) has to do only with being sensitive to the different realities of people from different cultures. We believe that competence as a professional from a cultural point of view, means much more than this. For a start, competent professionals need to be able to appreciate the skills and resources of a community, and the ways in which the particular community understands these. What is more, competent professionals then need to be able to play a part in assisting that person, or that community to engage with their own skills and knowledges in ways that contribute positively to their community" (Bracho & Latino Health Access 2000, p.7).

Honouring communities' cultural understandings of identity and mental health
The work of Kiwi Tamasese

The work of Kiwi Tamasese and the Just Therapy Team of Wellington, New Zealand, introduces further considerations when working across cultures. Their research illustrates the importance of honouring local cultural understandings of identity and mental health. More than this, they stress the importance of mental health interventions being based on the understandings of self of the local culture. Doing so requires a significant shift in the 'assessment' and 'provision' of mental health services:

"When the Samoan worldview meets with Western metaphors of mental health, they couldn't be more different and this has serious implications. Western science upholds a mind/body split and an individualistic conception of the self that is profoundly different from Samoan perspectives. Western medicine and the health professions are based on assumptions about the self that are rarely questioned and that are simply assumed to be the only ways of understanding life and health. What this often means is that when Samoan families in New Zealand are referred to mental health services in a crisis they can become more crazy rather than less. They find themselves in a situation in which there are two descriptions of reality, two descriptions of the self, which are in conflict with one another.

Within psychiatric services, the Western description of self has the upper hand and the Samoan families are treated accordingly. If the Samoan family tells the doctor about their alternative description of the problem - that they believe the symptoms being displayed could be due to a break in relationships with other people (living or no longer living), to breaches in protocol and etiquette, or to dislocation from land and a sense of belonging - they are likely to be dismissed and this dismissal can contribute to the person concerned becoming more crazy. What's more, the Samoan families' faith in their own belief system may be eroded and their cultural descriptions of life may become subjugated ...

Our main hope for this research is to invite mental health services to include not only the psychiatric / Western understanding of the self as the basis of their interventions, but when working with Samoan families to engage with, and indeed base their understandings around, Samoan conceptions of the self.

Mental health services for Samoan families need to be underpinned by Samoan conceptions of self, health and personhood. We certainly believe that certain aspects of western psychiatric understandings have a function within these services, but it is a limited function. Services need to be informed by the cultural understandings of the populations which they are designed to serve." (Tamasese 2002, pp.192-193)

Bali

Similar considerations of cultural meanings were highly relevant in the aftermath of the Bali bombing as local Balinese people tried to come to terms with this event and develop community responses that could contribute to healing. To read about these considerations see 'Voices from Bali: Responding to the October bombing' by Muhammad Arif, Putu Nur Ayomi, Janet De Neefe, Sugi B. Lanus, Ni Made Marni, Wayan Sarma and Frances Tse (2003).

To do no harm – avoiding psychological colonisation

In recent years, writers in the humanitarian aid field have sought to explore what it means to prioritise 'doing no harm' when delivering aid (Anderson 1999). This work has particularly focused on how to respond to situations of conflict in ways that do not exacerbate division or violence (see the work of Collaborative for Development Action http://www.cdainc.com/). The principles outlined above by Lara Perera relate to how international aid agencies can seek to 'do no harm' when they operate in Sri Lanka.

Similar considerations may be relevant in relation to the foreign provision of psychological services, counselling and other forms of mental health provision in times of crisis. After the tsunami a wide range of international organisations either offered support to Sri Lanka, or simply turned up and established counselling and other support services to local people. While the intent was to help, many local organisations had considerable concerns about the cultural appropriateness of the particular models and approaches that were being offered.

We have included here a set of questions that local organisations could ask foreign organisations who are offering psychological, counselling and/or other forms of mental health support. These questions have been designed to assist local organisations to gather information about the assumptions that inform the particular counselling or psychological approaches that are being offered by international organisations. It is hoped that clarifying these assumptions will enable a greater consideration of the implications that any particular approach many have for local communities and will reduce the likelihood of inadvertent psychological colonisation.

Articulating the cultural assumptions of psychological / counselling approaches:

What are the assumptions of this particular psychological of counselling model in relation to:

- *Identity*

  How does the approach understand identity? Is identity understood as residing solely within individuals, or also as a collective, social project? Is the approach designed for work only with individuals, or also with families, communities? What would be the implications for this particular context?

- *Trauma*

  Does the approach seek to build upon the cultural, collective, familial and individual skills in responding to and healing from experiences of trauma? Does it honour the histories of local knowledge in relation to trauma and healing? Does it have preconceived ideas as to what will be healing for a particular community? Does it define the experience of trauma and its meaning, or does it seek to consult community members on these matters? What would be the implications for this particular context?

- *Grief*

  Does the approach prescribe a 'right way' to respond to grief? Does it enquire about, honour and build upon collective, cultural, spiritual, familial and individual practices of remembrance? What would be the implications for this particular context?

- *Power/Neutrality*

  Does the approach believe that its practitioners can be neutral in their beliefs and actions? Or is there an acknowledgement that any approach brings with it certain assumptions and that every intervention involves considerations of power, culture, gender, class, etc?

- *Assessment*

  Does the approach 'assess' only the needs and problems of individuals and communities, or does it also seek to identify the skills and knowledge of local individuals, families and communities that can be used to address current difficulties? What would be the implications for this particular context?

• *Partnership*

Is it assumed that outsiders are capable of addressing problems facing the community or that partnerships are required to ensure that local cultural meanings and practices are respected? What would be the implications for this particular context?

We would be very interested in receiving feedback on this questionnaire. Please feel free to contact us c/o dulwich@senet.com.au

Final reflections

We hope that this collection of short pieces of writing conveys the degree of thoughtfulness that the local Sri Lankan organisations have been engaged in as they attempt to respond to the devastating effects of the tsunamis that struck their coastline on December 26th 2004. Alongside their work in the practical reconstruction of houses, villages, economic structures and their support and care of those most affected, they are also maintaining vigilance about avoiding the possible inadvertent negative effects of humanitarian aid delivery, and the imposition of western models of psychological understandings and responses to trauma.

We anticipate continuing conversations about the care required in cross-cultural disaster relief efforts. And we look forward to further contact between those involved in the work of humanitarian aid and those involved in responding to trauma through therapeutic and community work approaches.

Acknowledgements

Thanks to Shanti Arulampalam, Lara Perera, Sathis de Mel and Nalin Hemantha. Special thanks to Mathew Hyndes and Dhakshi Ariyakumar of the Australian High Commission in Colombo.

References

Arif, M., Nur Ayomi, P., De Neefe, J., Lanus, S. B., Made Marni, N., Sarma, W. & Tse, F. 2003: 'Voices from Bali: Responding to the October bombing.' *International Journal of Narrative Therapy and Community Work*, 1:75-80.

Anderson, M. 1989: *Rising From the Ashes: Development strategies in times of disaster*. Boulder: Westview Press.

Anderson, M. 1999: Do No Harm: *How aid can support peace – or war*. Boulder: Lynne Rienner Publishers.

Bracho, A. & Latino Health Access, 2000: 'Towards a healthy community ... even if we have to sell tamales. The work of Latino Health Access.' *Dulwich Centre Journal*, 3:3-20.

Elliott, C. 1999: *Locating the Energy for Change: An introduction to appreciative inquiry*. Winnipeg, Manitoba: International institute for sustainable development.

Hammond, S.A. 1998: *The Thin Book of Appreciative Inquiry*. Plano Texas: The Thin Book publishing.

Tamasese, K. 2002: 'Honouring Samoan ways and understandings: Towards culturally appropriate mental health services.' *International Journal of Narrative Therapy and Community Work*, 2:64-71. Republished 2003 in Waldegrave, C., Tamasese, K., Tuhaka, F. & Campbell, W. (eds): *Just Therapy – a journey: A collection of papers from the Just Therapy Team, New Zealand*, pp. 183-195 (chapter 12). Adelaide: Dulwich Centre Publications.

Further resources

For those interested in further reading about considerations in relation to Humanitarian Aid, we suggest the follow articles:

World Bank Policy Research Report Number 7: 'Assessing Aid: What Works, What Doesn't, and Why'. The International Bank for Reconstruction/World Bank. Oxford University Press, 1998-01-01. Available at: http://www.worldbank.org/research/aid/aidtoc.htm

'Humanitarian Aid and Development Assistance' by Amelia Branczik is available at http://www.intractableconflict.org/m/humanitarian_aid.jsp

A range of information is available at the website of Collaborative for Development Action: http://www.cdainc.com/

CHAPTER FOUR

Debriefing after traumatic situations

– using narrative ideas in the Gaza Strip

by Sue Mitchell

The concept of trauma de-briefing has been the focus of considerable debate in recent years. Are there ways in which narrative ideas can be helpful when meeting with people who have recently experienced trauma? This chapter describes the use of narrative ideas in debriefing Palestinian adults and children in the Gaza strip after traumatic experiences. The author was working as a volunteer psychologist for Medecins Sans Frontieres in Gaza.

A great part of my work as a psychologist for Medecins Sans Frontieres in the Gaza strip (mid 2004 - early 2005) involved responding to requests for therapy by Palestinian adults and children suffering the effects of ongoing violence, fear and sadness. There were occasions, however, when I was requested to debrief people directly after a particular traumatic experience. The practice of psychological debriefing is one that has become popular among relief agencies working within disaster settings and was considered a standard part of our work. And yet, the concept of debriefing was one that I had questions about. Long ago I had been exposed to the idea that debriefing meant providing an opportunity for people to retell the story of an horrific event and to re-engage with and express feelings associated with the event. In this single session, people were supposed to 'feel what they needed to feel' in a safe context, 'process their emotions' and be protected from later developing 'psychopathology' such as post traumatic stress disorder (PTSD). The debriefer could also 'normalise' the person's distress responses and provide techniques to manage these reactions. It is often advocated that this process be conducted in groups made up of people who have experienced the same traumatic experience (Mitchell 1983).

While I could see benefit in the idea of giving people the opportunity of having their story heard, their experience validated, I wondered about the potential for this debriefing to inadvertently re-traumatise a person. And, in the case of group debriefing, I wondered about the effects of exposure to other people's terrifying stories or experiences. Further, I considered that providing only one session without follow-up may leave people highly vulnerable. Indeed, many years ago working for an agency in Australia with people who had experienced torture, I regularly participated in worker group debriefing. In a wonderful attempt by the agency to take care of its workers, the most distressing and recurring memory of all that I heard while working there is that of a story told by one of my co-workers during a debriefing session.

Indeed, these same questions have been raised by many researchers and practitioners in recent years. The claim that single session debriefing can prevent later problems such as PTSD has been convincingly refuted and some argue that it can in fact impede natural recovery or make things worse (Rose et. al. 2002, Van Emmerik et. al. 2002). Problems considered by these researchers include the forced revisiting of the trauma, exposure to other's experiences and the insufficiency of a single session. The debate has been persuasive enough for the World Health Organisation to recommend against the dominant model of single session debriefing after disaster or emergency situations (WHO 2003).

It is argued however that some form of intervention is appropriate to relieve suffering and to attempt to prevent the development of psychological problems after experiences of trauma. WHO (2003) propose psychological 'first aid' within the context of a broader two-phase model focusing on social and practical assistance. The psychological first aid involves listening, conveying compassion, assessing needs, ensuring basic physical needs are met, not forcing talking, mobilising company and protecting from further harm. McFarlane (2003) however, argues that care and sympathy, although needed, are not enough and advocates that further interventions effective in preventing post-traumatic psychiatric problems are needed.

Consequently I was interested in alternatives to the dominant model of debriefing. It was my experience that people often wanted to talk about what had happened to them following a terrifying incident and did invite an audience to their experience. In meeting with people, my primary concern was to avoid retraumatisation. I became interested in how the person who had experienced trauma could be invited to re-tell their story from the perspective of a safer ground, a different territory of identity than that evoked by the traumatic experience.

I was interested in two lines of enquiry, both informed by narrative therapy ideas. The first involved questioning what any expression of distress signalled about what had been violated or devalued for the person. I became interested in exploring the values, beliefs, ideas, hopes or dreams that had been potentially dislodged by the traumatic experience. In this way I wanted to uncover what was 'absent but implicit' in the expressions of trauma (see White 2000) and to engage in conversations that made these values, beliefs, hopes or dreams available to the person again.

A second line of enquiry involved examining how the person survived the traumatic experience. I was interested in asking questions about the thoughts or actions that served to sustain him or her throughout the ordeal. I did not hold the hope that the value of the work lay in preventing the onset of PTSD or other 'pathology', but rather aimed to facilitate access to, and articulation of, skills and knowledges the person used to survive.

When offering debriefings for people in Gaza I didn't always manage to explore both of these enquiries fully, but they informed my thinking and led to some significant conversations. I will share here two stories of debriefings. The first occurred with a group of children and focused on the skills and knowledges they had developed in supporting each other during a major military attack. The second debriefing took place with an adult whose colleagues had been kidnapped. Our conversations explored some of the values that had been so powerfully violated during this kidnapping and the events that led up to it.

Finding ways to breathe - the children of the Aidini family

About ten children of the Aidini family and I were drawing faces in the sand of one of their uncle's backyards in the north of the Gaza Strip. The faces showed large inverted semi-circles for mouths and tears coming from their eyes. The children had fled from their neighbourhood a few days earlier during a heavy extended military operation where their homes had been surrounded by tanks, under fire, occupied or demolished by the Israeli Army. Managing to escape after twelve days, they were now staying with relatives in what they thought would be a safer place. However, the previous day and night had brought a new incursion, and again the children were subjected to tanks, helicopters, missiles and gun fire. The Israeli Army had now pulled out and I had been invited to 'debrief' the children who were keen to speak to me of their ordeal. Ayman, who is eight years old, told me 'I was feeling my heart small and I was unable to talk. I thought I was going to die'. As Ayman spoke, tears ran down his cheeks.

I asked Ayman about his tears and what they were an expression of. He said: 'When the people are dying, when houses are being destroyed, my tears are an alert'. I noted Ayman's words and then Aiya, a girl of ten, told me: 'I feel I am going to be killed here. I'm not able to breathe well'. I asked if anyone else was having difficulty breathing. The children were unanimous in their proclamation: 'Yes! All of us'. I asked the group what they thought was affecting their breathing. Answers included: 'When someone is killed', 'When the helicopters are there', 'When mines are planted', 'When our house is destroyed', 'When fields are razed'. I asked if these things had effects in addition to making it hard to breathe. The children told me that it was hard for them to eat or drink, that they often shake without control, that they cry a lot and can't sleep. They said they were too scared to go to school. The children agreed that there was a strong presence of fear and of sadness in their lives.

I asked the children about how they coped during the operation and how they coped when the tanks had left but sadness and fear were still present. One child said: 'We catch each other, we support each other'. I asked how they did this. Mohamed, eleven years old, told me the story of when a shell was launched and he saw his sister's face turn red and then she began to cry. He said: 'I talked to her'. Another tip was that it was important to 'keep our minds on the future, the day when we will be safe again'. Now that the operation was over the children told me that it was important to 'be together and to laugh', and to 'talk together'. They said one thing that helps is to think of games to play, like the one they offered to show me. The game involved breaking into two teams, lots of running around and rolling in the sandy ground. At the end of the game the children were panting and laughing. I asked the children if the game helps them breathe and they said it did.

I returned to the children about a week later. Ramadan had begun and people were generally attempting to honour the usual festive atmosphere that this brings. The children said that breathing had become easier since we last met. They named the kind of breath we were talking about, the Relief Breath. They told me about the times the Relief Breath was large - the first day of Ramadan and the day they felt safe enough to return to school. We explored the special powers of the Relief Breath and discovered that it helps the children to feel active, to play, to study and to eat. I asked the children to draw the Relief Breath in the sand and most of them drew big smiling faces. One boy, Mohamed, who was staying in a house a couple of blocks from the other children, told us that he continues to feel suffocated and unable to breathe. I asked others who were more in touch with the Relief Breath if they had any ideas for Mohamed. Hiba suggested: 'Come and play with us more, we don't see you much, it would be nice if you would come and play with us'. She also suggested that it would be better if he didn't visit the site of his demolished home, as he had been doing with his parents from time to time. I asked Mohamed what he thought about this idea and he said that it was much harder for him to breathe when he went there and that he did feel some relief when he didn't go. Hiba slapped me on the leg and smiled broadly; her theory was right! This led nicely to the proposition that we document the skills and knowledges of this group of people - to use for themselves should there be another attack, and also to pass on to other people in terrifying situations. The children thought this was a great idea. I had begun to draft a document from my notes of our last conversation and shared what I had recorded so far. The children approved what I had written and added some further ideas. Hiba said that she felt she would be able to manage an attack if it happened again, especially the not eating part, because Ramadan had trained her to be able to fast. A younger girl, Samah, said: 'Oh, I have another point to add. It's important to eat olives'. I asked her why. She said she wasn't sure and the group conversation continued. About ten minutes later, Samah said: 'Oh, I know why it's important to eat olives. It's because olive trees are the tree of peace'. The children pointed out, however, that their skills and knowledges in surviving a military attack were not so extraordinary: 'All Palestinian children know how to do these things'.

How to manage the effects of a military attack:
Tips for children from the children of the Aidini family

During the Attack

• It's important to support each other, to catch each other. Look at each other's faces, if you see that someone is distressed talk to him or her.

- Keep your mind on the future, imagine the day
  when you'll be safe again.
- If you have no food, remember Ramadan. It is possible to go
  for long periods without any food or drink.
- Practise patience.

After the Attack

- Make sure you have times to be together and laugh.
- Talk together.
- Invent games that make you laugh and help you breathe.
- Keep studying - this is a good way to fight.
- Practise patience - patience is the key to wellbeing.
- Care for each other. Invite kids who are suffering to
  play with you.
- Eat olives - the olive tree is the tree of peace.

Debriefing after a kidnapping - Ahmed's commitment to respect

I met Ahmed in the manicured gardens of the French Cultural Centre in Gaza city. The day before, four French associates of his had been kidnapped by members of an armed Palestinian resistance group and then released during the night. The French people were in Gaza as part of a sister city project with the southern Gaza city of Khan Younis. Ahmed was a primary member of the hosting group. The kidnappers had not taken Ahmed with the French people but he had remained outside the hotel in which they were held for the duration of the ordeal. Ahmed told me that it had been a terrifying afternoon and evening as the twenty or so armed and masked men controlled the situation, disallowing Ahmed access to his colleagues. When they were finally released, Ahmed followed his colleagues to the French Cultural Centre where they were now being cared for. My French speaking colleagues were debriefing the French people inside as I spoke outside with Ahmed. He told me that he was suffering deeply, that he felt responsible for what had happened. He hadn't been able to sleep or eat. Our conversation was interrupted by various media and administrative requests so I organised to meet Ahmed again some days later.

At our second meeting Ahmed told me that he couldn't believe that this had happened. He said he continued to suffer, had not been able to work and still had not been able to sleep or eat. He said that everything had 'stopped' for him. I didn't wish to have Ahmed recount the trauma of that night, his distress in relation to the event was obvious. Instead, I asked him what this suffering might say about what was important to him that has been denounced by the kidnapping. He said: 'For me, life is based on loving and respect for each other. Everyone has basic rights that are to be respected'. Ahmed wanted everyone to 'acknowledge and be committed to the notion of rights for all'. He said that the action of the kidnapping had failed to do this. It had violated the principles of respect for the rights of people that Ahmed treasured.

Ahmed expressed a second sadness. By now we were aware that the kidnapping had taken place in protest at the severe impoverishment faced by people living in the south of the Gaza where the kidnapping had taken place. This area is populated by refugee camps, sponsored by the United Nations Relief and Works Agency (UNRWA), in which people have been living since 1948. The French people had been mistaken for UNRWA diplomats and were kidnapped as an expression of outrage at the insufficient support of Palestinian refugees.

Ahmed told me that when basic rights are denied or are stolen from a person, 'for sure he will do his best to get them back. And this is what is going on in our life'. The kidnapping itself violated Ahmed's commitment to respecting everyone's rights. But he also saw that the actions of the kidnappers were an effect of the dishonouring of the rights of those in the refugee camps, and this too made him feel a great sadness.

I wanted to know more about Ahmed's values and how these had developed. By tracing the history of the values that had been violated by the traumatic experience, I hoped this would enable them to become more richly described. In turn, I hoped this would provide Ahmed an avenue to return to his original territory of identity. I hoped it would validate the significance of these values in his life.

Ahmed told me that the value of respect for everyone's rights had been with him a long time. He said it was taught to him as a child by his family and at school. He said the value is upheld in Islam. He gave me the example of the teaching of Islam to respect diversity of people and of religions - that this diversity is the intention of Allah: 'People here believe this, people there believe that, this is how it should be'. I reflected on the unequivocal respect I had been shown by Palestinian people during my time in Gaza, despite being non-Muslim and having different dress and behaviour practices.

He told me though that these values were further developed during his travels as a tertiary student. Ahmed had been able to travel outside Palestine, to other Arabic countries and to Spain. It was in these environments that he discovered a diversity of opinion and a delight in exchanging ideas with other people, to debate, and have different opinions respected. He was inspired by the diversity of ideas and how it was possible to be respectful of such diversity. Ahmed became more animated as he spoke of these student days, describing difference in landscapes, life styles, ideas, and the practice of debate.

Ahmed told me that he tries to 'distribute' these practices in his life in Gaza. I asked him more about this and he told me about different activities he was involved in. One activity he described was the sister city project - intended to promote exchange, respect and understanding between the people of the city of Khan Younis in the south of Gaza and the small French town from where the visitors had come. Despite the kidnapping, Ahmed was able to confirm that this long-standing project had managed to achieve its aim. There had been many delegations of people from the small French town come and stay in Palestinian homes. Some Palestinian children had also been able to visit France. And, he said, the project will continue.

He also told me about the Khan Younis Youth Activities Group on whose board Ahmed volunteers. The children who attend this group live in a very vulnerable area and have all had their homes demolished and at least one family member killed by the Israeli army. I heard how being connected to this group provides an opportunity for Ahmed to share his values and ideas with the children who attend and to promote the idea of respect despite such great hardship and loss.

In talking about these activities, I noticed that Ahmed was reconnecting with some of the key intentions that he has for his life. He was also recognising the ways in which he was enacting these intentions and values, and how his commitments were having a significant impact and influence.

In our conversations together, we had identified how the kidnapping had violated certain values that Ahmed holds dear. We explored the history of these values and examined the ways in which he was continuing to put these values into practice and the real effects of this on his life and the lives of others.

Having done so, our conversation came to a close and Ahmed told me, with a seemingly re-found resolve, that 'Life has to go on'. A few days later I spoke briefly to Ahmed. He told me he was back at work, finding sleep, eating again and planning the next visit of his French colleagues.

Conclusion

In writing this piece I am hopeful that ideas around debriefing after trauma will be further explored. I think that as therapists we can be useful in offering support to people soon after a terrifying event by reinvigorating what it is a person holds dear or by making people's particular skills and knowledges accessible to them again. I would welcome conversations with others who have been working in similar situations. Finally, I feel privileged to have had the opportunity of engaging in rich and inspiring conversations with people in the Gaza Strip. In sharing these stories I hope that some of the inspiration I was afforded is also shared.

Words from Khan Younis Youth Activities Group

Following our conversations, Ahmed invited me to meet with the children and teenagers of the Khan Younis Youth Activities Group. About twenty girls and boys were eager to speak with me of their experiences of violence and loss and engaged with me in mapping the effects of violence, fear and sadness on their lives. The focus of the conversation, however, soon turned to the presence of Hope and how the children managed to stay connected to Hope despite everything that had happened. Halfway through our conversation we were interrupted by loud gun fire from the Israeli Army watchtower nearby. Once the shooting stopped and we were able to speak again, one of the boys, now versed in my narrative style inquiry, asked me: 'So how does the gun fire affect you?' I laughed and then told him that during the shooting I felt Fear, but also Anger. I asked the children if Anger was also around for them. The boy laughed and said 'Oh, yes, we know Anger, but we don't hold on to Anger'. I asked about this and he told me: 'Well, if you go with Anger, you will only feel terrible. If you stay with Hope you can continue to study, to laugh, to live.'

Acknowledgements

Sincere thanks to David Denborough, Cheryl White, Shona Russell, Maggie Carey and Mark Hayward for their insights, reflections, ideas and support during my time in Gaza, and to Kaethe Weingarten for reflections and advice on this article.

References

McFarlane, A. C. 2003: 'Debriefing: Care and sympathy are not enough.' *Medical Journal of Australia,* 178 (11).

Mitchell, J. T. 1983: 'When disaster strikes: The critical incident stress debriefing process.' *Journal of Emergency Medical Service,* 8 (1).

Rose, S, Bisson, J, Churchill, R, & Wessely, S. 2004: 'Psychological debriefing for preventing PTSD'. *The Cochrane Library,* Issue 2. Chichester, UK: Wiley.

Van Emmerik, A. A., Kamphuis J. H., Hulsbosch A. M., & Emmelkamp P. M. 2002: 'Single session debriefing after psychological trauma: A meta analysis.' *Lancet,* 360 (9335).

White, M. 2000: 'Re-engaging with history: The absent but implicit.' In White, M.: *Reflections on Narrative Practice: Essays & interviews* (chapter 3), pp.35-58. Adelaide: Dulwich Centre Publications.

World Health Organisation, 2003: 'Mental health in emergencies: mental and social aspects of health of populations exposed to extreme Stressors.' *Department of Mental Health and Substance Dependence.* WHO: Geneva.

CHAPTER FIVE

A framework for receiving and documenting testimonies of trauma

by David Denborough

This chapter seeks to provide a framework for receiving and documenting the testimonies of those who have been subjected to trauma, violence and abuse. It is a framework designed to make it possible to receive and document testimonies in ways that are not re-traumatising and that, in fact, contribute to redressing the effects of trauma in the person's life. The testimonies that are created can then be used for broader purposes.

There are many different contexts in which testimonies of trauma are received and documented. Therapists may invite those who consult with them to re-tell the stories of abuse or trauma that they have been subjected to, and these may be recorded in case files and/or in therapeutic letters or documents. The legal system requires the 'taking of testimonies' from those seeking legal redress and these are documented in particular ways. And in different parts of the world, especially those where human rights violations are widespread, various organisations are documenting the testimonies of those who seek counselling assistance[1]. They are doing so in the hope that this will provide some relief to the person's experience of the trauma, and also so that these testimonies can be used for broader purposes – to raise awareness of human rights violations at the United Nations, or in the International Criminal Court in the Hague.

Over the past few years, I have spoken with a wide range of people involved in each of these different domains – with therapists and lawyers, and with workers in trauma and torture centres and women's rights centres, in Bangladesh, Lebanon, South Africa, Israel, the Palestinian Territories, Australia, and elsewhere. The conversations we have shared about receiving and documenting testimonies have been startling. A number of human rights organisations have stopped taking testimonies entirely because they realised that they had been inadvertently re-traumatising the very people they were seeking to assist. And a range of therapists told alarming stories of how their work with a particular person (often women) was derailed through the person's involvement in a legal proceeding. The act of publicly re-telling their story of trauma in particular ways had led to a significant resurgence of despair and hopelessness in these people's lives. This paper has been written in response to these conversations.

It has also been written in the context of my work as staff writer at Dulwich Centre Publications. Part of this work involves interviewing and documenting the stories of individuals and communities who have experienced significant trauma. Significantly, we do more than only document the experience of trauma. We also document the ways in which these individuals and communities have responded to this trauma, their initiatives, their acts and skills of resistance and healing, their hopes and values, and the histories of these hopes and values. As a result, the testimonies that are created can be understood to be 'double-storied testimonies'[2].

Mostly this work involves documenting stories in the written word. But on various occasions we work in collaboration with people who have been subjected to considerable abuse in order for them to be able to re-tell their experiences in public settings, such as international conferences, in ways that will involve the sharing of their particular knowledge and skills[3]. Sometimes testimonies can also be documented in song[4].

This paper seeks to provide a possible framework for receiving and documenting the testimonies of those who have been subjected to trauma, violence and abuse. It's my hope that this framework will assist others to receive and document testimonies in ways that are not re-traumatising and that, in fact, contribute to redressing the effects of trauma in the person's life. The documents that are created can then be used for broader purposes including:

- to share with others who have been through similar experiences;

- to educate professionals about the skills and knowledge of those who have survived traumatic experiences;

- to raise community awareness about the effects of trauma and violence in order to play a part in reducing the likelihood of further abuses;

- to facilitate broader political/community action;

- to seek forms of individual or social acknowledgement;

- to seek formal redress/justice.

It is my experience that it is possible to create contexts in which the receiving and documentation of testimonies can provide significant relief and comfort to the individual or community concerned, and at the same time produce powerful documentation which can be used for all the purposes listed above.

An easy-to-use framework

In the following pages I have deliberately tried to describe a very easy-to-use framework[5]. In visiting various human rights centres in different parts of the world, I have come to realise that the people who are taking these testimonies have often received no formal training in this area. Significantly, they bring with them their own knowledge and experience of trauma and surviving trauma. They bring with them a profound commitment to the people who walk in the doors to meet with them. It is my sincere hope that the framework provided below might be of relevance to their work. It is a framework that can be followed through in only three meetings because I have been told that this is sometimes the maximum length of time that is available.

Four key hopes have guided the development of this framework for receiving and documenting testimonies related to experiences of trauma. Firstly, to create a process of documenting people's testimonies that can be understood to be both political action and a contribution to therapeutic and community work. Secondly, to avoid re-traumatisation. Thirdly, to create a process of receiving and documenting testimonies that contributes to healing. Fourthly, to create richly described testimonies that can serve many purposes.

It is possible to create testimonies that document the abuse/ torture/trauma that a person has been subject to, and also the ways in which they have resisted these abuses, held onto hopes, and reclaimed their lives from the effects of the trauma. These dual or double storied testimonies can be of significant benefit to the person who gives the testimony. They can also be shared with others who have been through similar experiences, used in training contexts, and used to raise awareness as forms of broader social and political action[6].

A framework for receiving testimonies in relation to experiences of trauma

I will now outline a step-by-step process in relation to receiving testimonies in relation to experiences of trauma. This process consists of:

- Preparing the person for the interview.

- Setting a context of care at the beginning of the interview.

- A three part interviewing process.

- Offering an acknowledgement / reflection at the end of the interview.

- Writing up the testimony.

- A second meeting with the person who gave the testimony.

- Follow-up.

Each of these steps will now be considered.

Preparing the person for the interview

Preparing the person who is to give their testimony is significant in itself. Prior to someone giving their testimony they can be asked where and how would be best for them to be interviewed. They can be asked if they would like to bring with them a friend, family member, and/or therapist. Where possible, a written invitation can be provided that describes the purpose of creating the testimony, why it will be significant, how it will contribute to the lives of others.

If the work is taking place in a context in which many of the people who give their testimonies will have been interrogated in the past, it can be significant for them to know prior to the interview who they will be meeting with and even to receive some of the questions beforehand. This can assist people to familiarise themselves with the kinds of questions to be asked, and how these differ radically from the questioning techniques associated with interrogation.

It is important for the person to know that, if there are any questions they do not wish to answer that this is completely okay, they can decide not to answer them, they can decide to take a break, or even stop the process entirely at any time. It can also be significant for them to receive detailed information about who will hear their testimony, who will read it, and how confidentiality will be maintained. If formal consent forms need to be considered, this is the time to do so. It is also relevant at this point to outline what follow-up, if any, will be provided[7].

Setting a context of care at the beginning of the interview

When the actual interview begins, there are a number of practices of care that can make a significant difference to how the process is experienced by the person giving their testimony. For instance, at the outset it can be acknowledged that this testimony will make a difference to others: that it will raise awareness; assist others who have been through similar experiences; and so on.

It can be acknowledged before the interview begins that the person who is about to give their testimony has been through traumatic experiences but also that they have survived the experience. It can be explained that this process of receiving testimonies involves speaking about both the effects of the trauma that they experienced, and also how they have been able to survive it – the skills and knowledge they have developed that they can pass onto others.

It can also be acknowledged that giving testimony like this is a very significant thing to do, that the conversation to be shared will touch upon different stories of the person's life. The person who is about to give their testimony can be consulted about how they could know if the conversation was getting to be too much, how they could let the interviewer know if this was the case, and what would be most helpful if this occurred. Certain options can be suggested, such as: taking a short break; having a cup of tea; having a smoke; taking a walk; having a moment's quiet; stopping for the time being and coming back another day; stopping altogether and not going through with the process; and so on. Collaboratively, the interviewer and the person who is to give their testimony can pre-empt any difficulties and develop some proposals as to ways to respond to these.

As part of this process, the interviewer can mention that they will regularly check-in with the person about how they are experiencing the interview, about whether it is going okay, whether it would be good to pause for a moment, or to continue, and so on.

A three part interviewing process

I have often been asked to develop a standard interviewing format that could be used to receive testimonies from those who have experienced trauma. This can be important in order to be transparent about the process (and to gain acceptance amongst legal circles), and it is also reassuring to those who are new to receiving and documenting testimonies. I have outlined here the sorts of questions that can be included within a three part interview format.

Part One (setting a context)

- Can you share with us some of your hopes in giving this testimony today? Why have you decided to do this?

- What does this say about what is important to you, about what you care about and value in life?

- Have these things always been important to you? What is the history of this?

- Who would be least surprised to know that you have decided to give testimony today? Why? What do they know about you that would mean they wouldn't be surprised to see you here today?

Part Two (documenting the abuse/torture and its effects)

- Can you tell us about the trauma/torture that you were subject to? Did these abuses take different forms?

- During the time when you were being subjected to this injustice, how did you try to endure this? What did you try to think about? Were there any memories you tried to hold onto? Any dreams? What sustained you through these most awful times?

- Were there different ways that you tried to endure the different forms of torture/trauma?

- Why it is important to you for other people to know about this?

- What were the effects of these forms of trauma/torture in your life? What were the effects on you? On your relationships? On your family? On your community?

- What were some of the most difficult effects for you? Why were these the most difficult?

- Are there any ongoing effects of this trauma/torture in your life?

Part Three (eliciting stories of survival/resistance)

- At the beginning of this interview you spoke about those things that are important to you in your life (repeat whatever these were). How have you been able to keep in touch with these values, these hopes for your life, despite the abuses that you were subjected to?

- Have there been ways in which you have been able to reduce the effects of the traumas in your life? If so, how have you done this? Are these ways of reducing the effects of trauma newly developed? Or have they been around in your life for some time? What is their history?

- Have there been particular people who have made a difference? If so, what is it that they have done or said that has been significant to you? Why was this significant to you?

- If someone else went through similar experiences to you, what suggestions would you offer them? What stories could you tell them that would convey some of the steps you have taken to reclaim your life from the effects of this trauma?

Offering an acknowledgement / reflection at the end of the interview

It makes a considerable difference to people who give testimony if, at the end of telling the stories of their experience, they receive a significant response from the interviewer[8]. This response can focus on the contribution that the person's testimony will make to others; how it has taught the interviewer something; how the ideas and knowledge the person has shared will be of assistance to others. This acknowledgement/reflection can focus on the skills that the person has described and the stories of how they have reclaimed aspects of their life[9]. If the interviewer is able to re-tell some of the key aspects of the testimony that were most significant to them; why these particular aspects resonated; what these aspects of the story of survival indicated to them about the values and beliefs of the person whose testimony has been described; and how hearing this testimony has in some way influenced them; how it will bring about some change in their own life, work or way of seeing the world; then this can make a significant difference to the experience of the person who has offered the testimony. Such reflections, which are also known as outsider-witness responses, can reinforce for the person who has offered their testimony that the experience of trauma was 'not for nothing' and, as well, that giving the testimony has been worthwhile and honourably received.

Writing up the testimony

In writing up the testimony, it is important to keep in mind that the person who told their stories will be offered an opportunity to read the document. In taking this into account, it makes a real difference if the documentation of the testimony balances the story of the torture/trauma with the story of the person's resistance/survival/healing. It is significant if these can have an equal focus.

In documenting the stories of trauma there are three key aspects to be included:

1. The events themselves, what the person was subject to.

2. The effects of these events. These effects can be traced in terms of the effects on the person and their sense of identity, the effects on their relationships, and the effects on the wider community.

3. The person's responses to the trauma and what these indicate in relation to the person's hopes, values and wishes for their life.

Even throughout the first half of the testimony, where the experiences of trauma are discussed, it is necessary to include the person's responses to the trauma. For instance, when someone has been imprisoned, there will have been ways in which they acted when in prison to try to keep up their spirits, or assist others, or memories they will have held onto, etc. Where it is appropriate, considerations of how they held onto hope and didn't give up on their lives can be included. Recording these responses to the trauma throughout the testimony is a significant part of the process of 'dual testimony'. This rich description of the person's practices of resistance and survival can then be extended in the second part of the documented testimony.

The second half of the written testimony is to contain stories of the skills and knowledge of the person about how they coped with the trauma, how they responded, what has been significant in reclaiming their life, what is significant to them now, and how they are taking steps to live the sort of life they want to live.

Creating written testimonies that can be used in a range of contexts (so the person themselves can read it; so that they can be sent to United Nations; so that other people and communities who have been through trauma find them helpful; so that they can be used to train professionals, etc.) can be challenging. However, when testimonies are created with only a professional or judicial audience in mind, this alters the entire process of receiving and responding to testimony. It also alters the language that is used in the documentation. There are ways of writing up the effects of trauma that describe these vividly and powerfully, while not using psychiatric terms. Often this means that non-experts will engage more with the testimonies. Often it also means that the written testimony becomes increasingly meaningful to the person themselves. Formal documents can be created while still including, and staying true to, the actual words used by the person whose story is being told.

Second meeting with the person who gave the testimony

Once the testimony has been documented, it is then appropriate to arrange a second meeting with the person. In this second meeting the written testimony is shared with the person. She or he can be asked if the written document is accurate, and they can make any changes or additions in order for it to be finalised. They can also be asked for feedback on the process, whether it was a good process to give the testimony and to read the document, and if they have any suggestions that could make it better. They can be asked if there is anything they would like to pass on to others who are considering taking the step of giving testimony, that might help these people decide and/or prepare for the experience. The person can then be given a copy of their testimony and a certificate of acknowledgement[10]. This formal certificate explicitly acknowledges the person's actions and their contribution, through providing their testimony, to the lives of others. Where appropriate, a formal ceremony can be held in which the final version of testimony is read aloud in front of a group of key supportive figures and the certificate is presented.

Follow-up

Whatever follow-up has been arranged and described at the outset of the process needs to then be put in place. As mentioned earlier, it is of great importance that any commitment to follow-up that has been promised does take place.

Reflections on this framework

The structure I have outlined here is only one possible framework for receiving and documenting testimonies. It is a framework that would need to be adjusted depending upon the local cultural context. It does however, I believe, provide some helpful pointers as to ways of eliciting and recording testimonies of experiences of trauma that minimise the risk of re-traumatisation.

The process outlined above involves: preparing people for the interview in certain ways; asking certain questions; responding to the person's testimony in particular ways; and creating the document with attention to particular matters. Significantly, this process involves taking the document back to the person who has given the testimony and checking that it accurately records their experience. The process is completed by a ceremony of social acknowledgement for the person who has given their testimony. We have found that all these factors can create a context in which the documentation of a person's testimony can be profoundly healing.

Broader considerations

By no means do I wish to suggest that the task of revising the ways in which people's testimonies are sought and received will be easy. Within legal circles, there are powerful traditions and assumptions about what can constitute 'uncontaminated' testimony, about how some processes of questioning are 'neutral' while others are 'leading'. There are powerful conventions as to what sorts of testimonies are 'acceptable' and 'valid'. There are also conventions that encourage the telling and re-telling (and even the escalation) of stories of 'personal damage' incurred by trauma as the degree of 'damage' that has been done to a person routinely corresponds to the compensation that is then dispensed[11]. All these conventions influence how testimonies are elicited and documented. All these conventions have real effects on the lives and identities of those who offer their testimonies.

There are also influential conventions within the therapy world in general, and the trauma field more particularly, that regularly invite people to recount their experiences in ways that re-traumatise, or that contribute to identity conclusions of damage, pathology or fragility. I am sure that readers of this book are more than familiar with these conventions and so I will not further describe these here.

What I will mention, however, are a number of alternative voices appearing within the trauma field that may make it more likely for 'double-storied' testimonies to gain greater acceptance. The work of Summerfield (1995) and Becker (1995) for instance are drawing attention to the limitations of individualised western psychiatric knowledge in the field of trauma, are questioning the effects of victimology, and are inviting greater attention and respect to be paid to cultural meanings of both trauma and survival. Practitioners from non-western perspectives are also questioning psychological approaches to trauma work (see Arulampalam et al. 2005). At the same time, some feminist psychologists are rigorously questioning the ways in which women's stories/testimonies are attended to and re-told. While acknowledging the very real effects of violence and abuse, Sharon Lamb (1999) eloquently attempts to disrupt descriptions that locate women as passive victims, and to move discussions of abuse out from the realm of individual mental health and back into a political and social-cultural realm.

She writes: 'In changing the focus, we would also no longer be interested merely in women telling their stories of abuse but rather would encourage their stories of everyday resistance.' (p.33)

Significantly, there are voices within the legal realm that are also seeking alternative ways forward. Indigenous communities here in Australia, in Canada and elsewhere, continue to propose alternatives to mainstream legal systems (see Behrendt 1995, 2002; Gatensky 1996; Kelly 2002). Within these alternatives there is room for a different sort of sharing of stories and testimonies. At the same time, feminist lawyers, writers and activists continue to draw attention to the real effects of certain legal and trial processes for women who have been subjected to abuse and violence[12]. And in response to these sorts of experiences, some feminist psychologists and lawyers are examining the possibilities and hazards of alternative community-based forms of justice in relation to crimes of violence against women. Two invigorating examples of such feminist explorations include Koss (2000) and Rubin (2003).

It is my hope that providing this alternative framework for receiving and documenting testimonies can contribute in some small way to these continuing attempts to find alternative ways of responding to experiences of trauma and violence. I hope that this framework may provide a basis for practitioners, whether therapists, community workers, lawyers, or activists, to develop their own ways of receiving and documenting testimonies that do not re-traumatise those whose stories are being shared, that instead honour the richness of these 'dual testimonies', and that enable these testimonies to be shared widely.

Acknowledgements

The following people all offered feedback on an earlier draft: Sheridan Linnell, Vanessa Jackson, Patrick Moss, Fr Michael Lapsley, Taimalie Kiwi Tamasese, Shona Russell, Angela Tsun on-kee, Maggie Carey, Mark Hayward, Yvonne Sliep, Sue Mann, Elias Wanyama, Emile Makhlouf & Charles Waldegrave. Michael White's ideas in relation to double-storied responses to trauma are obviously key to this paper. So too are the principles of documentation and publishing, and considerations of the politics of representation, developed by Cheryl White.

Notes

1. Some of this work has been influenced by the work of Chilean psychologists Cienfuegos & Monelli (1983) and the work of Agger & Jensen (1990) and Herman (1992). Other testimonies are being documented according to strict legal frameworks provided by the United Nations or International Criminal Court in the Hague.

2. See the work of Michael White (2004) for explanations of the significance of eliciting double-stories in relation to experiences of trauma.

3. At the end of this paper a list is provided of examples of these double-storied testimonies in relation to experiences of trauma.

4. See Denborough (2002).

5. In order to ensure that this framework is easy to engage with, I have not included within it some of the other key narrative therapy concepts that can be highly relevant in this area of trauma work. For instance, I have not included descriptions of the use of the notion of the 'absent but implicit' (see White 2000). I have also written this framework as if it is to be used with individuals. The same framework, however, can be used to document the testimonies of groups or communities.

6. Significantly, these sorts of dual testimonies are much more engaging for readers than single-storied accounts of trauma. Whereas outside audiences are likely to only read a small number of testimonies that only tell the story of the trauma, if double stories can be told, the testimonies often begin to have a life of their own and are much more widely distributed. The influence of the testimonies in creating broader change is therefore much greater.

7. What is of critical importance is that the process is transparent and that no promises are made that will not be able to be kept. Raising expectations beyond that which will be able to be delivered is very unhelpful.

8. In some circumstances it might be easier or more appropriate for a third person or persons to offer this reflection when the giving of testimony is complete. Involving others who have been through similar traumatic experiences in this role can be significant.

9. There is a wealth of literature about these sorts of outsider-witness responses and what makes it more likely for these to resonate and be experienced as acknowledging by the person who has given the testimony. For further information about these sorts of acknowledging responses see Michael White's descriptions of outsider-witness responses (1999).

10. In some circumstances, it may not be safe for people to possess a certificate that acknowledges their testimony to an official organisation. If this is the case, an alternative form of acknowledgement can be created, one that does not explicitly refer to the fact that the person has given testimony but instead acknowledges certain attributes and contributions that the person has made.

11. Basing compensation on degrees of damage done to a person is only one possible configuration of justice. Alternative methods could include linking compensation payments to categories of injustice done, rather than damage done. While the development of such

categories of injustice would be complex and fraught, it could provide an antidote to people needing to prove the degree of damage they have sustained in order to receive compensation which runs the risk of escalating distress and prioritising the re-telling of single-storied accounts of trauma.

12. For instance, here in Australia, the Department for Women has drawn attention to the distress caused to women by sexual assault trial processes:

In 65% of trials there were, on average, two interruptions to evidence because of the distress suffered by complainants. This occurred more often for complainants with disabilities and complainants from Aboriginal communities. (1996, p.4)

More recently, Dr Mary Heath (2005) has illustrated the continuing very real effects of certain legal processes on the lives of women who have been sexually assaulted:

The very systems that Australia has implemented to respond to criminal conduct are still judged inappropriate or unusable by many people who are sexually assaulted yet never report their experiences to the police ... Those who do use the criminal justice system continue to find it traumatising, humiliating and distressing ... The process does not adequately recognise and respect the community service that complainant witnesses provide in reporting offences and participating in trials ... (p.31)

References

Agger, I. & Jensen, S.B. 1990: 'Testimony as ritual and evidence in psychotherapy for political refugees.' *Journal of Traumatic Stress,* 3:115-30.

Arulampalam, S., Perera, L., de Mel, S., White, C. & Denborough, D. 2005: 'Stories from Sri Lanka – responding to the tsunami.' *International Journal of Narrative Therapy and Community Work #2.*

Becker, D. 1995: 'The deficiency of the concept of posttraumatic stress disorder when dealing with victims of human rights violations.' In Kleber, R., Figley, C. & Gersons, B. (Eds): *Beyond Trauma: Cultural and social dynamics.* New York: Plenum Press.

Behrendt, L. 1995: *Aboriginal Dispute Resolution: A step towards self-determination and community autonomy.* Sydney: The Federation Press.

Behrendt, L. 2002: 'Lessons from the mediation obsession: Ensuring that sentencing 'alternatives' focus on indigenous self-determination.' In Strang, H. & Braithwaite, J. (Eds): *Restorative Justice and Family Violence.* Cambridge: Cambridge University Press.

Cienfuegos, J. & Monelli, C. 1983: 'The testimony of political repression as a therapeutic instrument', *American Journal of Orthopsychiatry,* 53:43-51.

Denborough, D. 2002: 'Community song-writing and narrative practice.' *Clinical Psychology,* 17:17-24.

Department for Women, 1996: *Heroines of Fortitude: The experiences of women in court as victims of sexual assault.* Gender Bias and the Law Project. NSW: Department for Women.

Heath, M. 2005: 'The law and sexual offences against adults in Australia.' *Australian Centre for the Study of Sexual Assault Issues Paper, #4, June.* Melbourne: Australian Institute of Family Studies.

Gatensky, H. 1996: 'Circle Justice.' In Denborough, D. (Ed): *Beyond the Prison: Gathering dreams of freedom.* Adelaide: Dulwich Centre Publications.

Herman, J. 1992: *Trauma and Recovery: The aftermath of violence – From domestic abuse to political torture.* New York: Basic Books.

Koss, M. 2000: 'Blame, shame, and community justice responses to violence against women.' *American Psychologist,* November.

Lamb, S. 1999: 'Constructing the victim: Popular images and lasting labels.' In Lamb, S. (Ed): *New Versions of Victims: Feminists struggle with the concept.* New York: New York University Press.

Rubin, P. 2003: *Restorative Justice in Nova Scotia: Women's experience and recommendations for positive policy development and implementation. Report and recommendations.* Ottawa, Canada: National Association of Women and the Law.

Kelly, L. 2002: 'Using restorative justice principles to address family violence in Aboriginal communities.' In Strang, H. & Braithwaite, J. (Eds): *Restorative Justice and Family Violence.* Cambridge: Cambridge University Press.

Summerfield, D. 1995: 'Addressing human response to war and atrocity: Major challenges in research and practices and the limitations of western psychiatric models.' In Kleber, R., Figley, C. & Gersons, B. (Eds): *Beyond Trauma: Cultural and social dynamics.* New York: Plenum Press.

White, M. 1999: 'Reflecting-team work as definitional ceremony revisited.' *Gecko: a journal of deconstruction and narrative ideas in therapeutic practice,* 2:55-82. Republished 2000 in White, M.: *Reflections on Narrative Practice: Essays & interviews* (chapter 4), pp.59-85. Adelaide: Dulwich Centre Publications.

White, M. 2000: 'Re-engaging with history: The absent but implicit.' In White, M.: *Reflections on Narrative Practice: Essays & interviews* (chapter 3), pp.35-58. Adelaide: Dulwich Centre Publications.

White, M. 2004: 'Working with people who are suffering the consequences of multiple trauma: A narrative perspective.' *International Journal of Narrative Therapy and Community Work* #1.

EXAMPLES OF DOUBLE-STORIED TESTIMONIES

For examples of 'double-storied testimonies' in relation to experiences of trauma, see the following:

Amir, 2001: 'Still searching.' *Dulwich Centre Journal*, 1:22-23.

Bullimore, P. 2003: 'Altering the balance of power: working with voices.' *International Journal of Narrative Therapy and Community Work*, 3:22-28.

Nicholls, C. 1998: 'A story of survival.' *Dulwich Centre Journal*, Nos.2&3. Republished 1999 in Dulwich Centre Publications (Eds): *Extending Narrative Therapy: A collection of practice-based papers* (chapter 9), pp.117-124. Adelaide: Dulwich Centre Publications.

de Valda, M. 2003: 'From paranoid schizophrenia to hearing voices – and other class distinctions.' *International Journal of Narrative Therapy and Community Work*, 3:13-17.

Kathy, 1999: 'Experiences of homelessness: From an interview (Denborough, D. & White, C. interviewers).' *Dulwich Centre Journal*, 3:2-8.

Mia, 1998: 'Resilience is a beautiful word.' *Dulwich Centre Journal*, 4:18-20.

O'Neill, M. 2004: 'Researching "suicidal thoughts" and archiving young people's insider knowledges.' *International Journal of Narrative Therapy and Community Work*, 3:38-40.

Sheedy, L. 2005: 'Try to put yourselves in our skin: The experiences of Wardies and Homies.' *International Journal of Narrative Therapy and Community Work*, 1:65-71.

Silent Too Long, 2000: 'Embracing the old, nurturing the new.' *Dulwich Centre Journal*, 1&2:62-71. Republished 2003 in Dulwich Centre Publications (Eds): *Responding to Violence: A collection of papers relating to child sexual abuse and violence in intimate relationships*, pp.71-91 (chapter 3). Adelaide: Dulwich Centre Publications.

Silent Too Long, 1998: 'Your voices inspire mine.' *Dulwich Centre Journal*, 4:2-8.

The Narrandera Koori Community 2002: 'The Narrandera Koori Community Gathering' *www.dulwichcentre.com.au*

Wingard, B. & Lester, J. (Eds) 2001: *Telling Our Stories in Ways that Make Us Stronger*. Adelaide: Dulwich Centre Publications.

WOWSafe, 2002: 'Seeking safety and acknowledgement.' *International Journal of Narrative Therapy and Community Work*, 1:70-74. Republished 2003 in Dulwich Centre Publications (Eds): *Responding to Violence: A collection of papers relating to child sexual abuse and violence in intimate relationships*, pp.129-138 (chapter 7). Adelaide: Dulwich Centre Publications.

CHAPTER SIX

Responding to families at times of trauma:

personal and professional knowledge

an interview with Yael Gershoni

In this chapter, Yael Gershoni, an Israeli therapist, tells the story of how a suicide bombing affected her relative's family and how this, in turn, has influenced her life and work. Particular emphasis is given to ways of responding to the traumatic visual imagery that is often an after effect of experiences of trauma. The interviewer was David Denborough.

Yael, I know that in recent times your family has been personally affected by trauma and that you have needed to find ways of responding to this alongside your regular work as a therapist. We really appreciate that you are going to speak about some of these experiences and how they have influenced your understandings about ways of responding to families in trauma. Would it be most appropriate to start by describing the events of your family's trauma ... ?

The bombing occurred when the two parents and the grandmother were sitting with the baby, Sinai, in a small ice-cream parlour. At the time, they were living in a small neighbourhood mainly of young families and plenty of children. After work, the parents had taken Sinai with Sinai's grandmother to buy some ice-cream and this was when the suicide bomber came. They remembered that when the suicide bomber arrived he went to stand very close to the baby carriage before blowing himself up. Sinai was thrown from the carriage onto the sidewalk. As soon as the father had picked himself up, he carried Sinai to a paramedic who had arrived quickly, but he knew that she was very badly wounded. He then went back and spoke to Sinai's grandmother and she responded to him before he ran to find his wife. When he came back, Sinai's grandmother had died.

The surviving adults were taken to hospital, although not in the same ambulance. The baby had been taken earlier. When they awoke after surgery my daughter called me (she is related by marriage to Sinai's father). My daughter already knew that Sinai had died and the grandmother had died, but the parents did not yet know this. I was asked to come to the hospital to help them tell the parents. When I arrived, I saw my daughter and the mother of Sinai's father. The social worker came to speak with us and told us that Sinai's mother would be out from the operation very soon and they wanted us to let her know and then to go with her to tell her husband. He was the most wounded so they thought it would be best if he heard the news from his wife. So we sat together and discussed how to let Sinai's mother know. She had lost her mother and her baby who was one year and two months old. After discussing it, we decided that the social worker and her mother-in-law would approach Sinai's mother, while I stood to one side.

I soon heard Sinai's mother screaming: 'I want to see my husband', and so they took her immediately. Sinai's parents were moved into a room together and, while they were too weak to stand, they held hands across their beds for one week. She told her husband that their child and her mother had died.

Ever since, I have tried to think about ways of telling people the worst possible news. I still do not have clear answers, but if possible I think I would like to be surrounded by love, and I would also like to be asked about what would be best for me. For some people it might be best to hear the worst news from family members. For others, it might be best to hear from a professional, someone not so close to the stories of their lives.

When we were talking earlier, Yael, you mentioned some of the things that have changed for you since these events, your perceptions of the world, some of the things that you have learnt from this sorrow ... would you be able to speak about some of this here?

What have I learned from all of this? As I have watched this family struggle to put their life back together? First of all, I have learned that it takes a much longer time than I thought to survive a trauma like that. I didn't have in my imagination an understanding of the desolation brought by events like this, of how it is possible that these events can break your life. To reclaim a sense of purpose can be so slow, so many small steps over years and years. I didn't really know this.

Another thing I have learned is that events like this affect everyone. I have seen how this bombing has affected my daughter, my grandchildren, my son-in-law, and of course the parents and grandparents of the baby. Two months ago we had a birthday celebration for my daughter. We went to a restaurant in Jerusalem and were having a great time. I looked at my son-in-law, however, and realised that there was no smile on his face. I asked him quietly what was wrong and he said that he was so afraid that any minute a suicide bombing would take place. He said that he can no longer enjoy himself at any public parade or celebration because he is frightened that something will happen to his loved ones. Now, whenever I hear of violence and loss of life, I think of all those who will be affected so powerfully, and for many years.

On the other hand, I now also have a richer admiration for the ways in which people rebuild their lives after tragedy. To lose your mother and baby on the same day is hard to imagine. But this was three-and-a-half years ago now and I have watched Sinai's mother take small steps towards a new life. She has a son now and is pregnant again with another child. She is still struggling with how to live and the loss of Sinai is ever-present. But they are also living, and Sinai's presence remains with them through good times and bad. They left Israel as soon as they recovered physically and they now live in the USA, but they come back to visit Israel. They meet their friends and work to build a richer life.

I have also been powerfully moved by how children have responded to this tragedy. We still visit the ice-cream parlour where it took place. It is the only ice-cream place in this neighbourhood and it gets very hot here! One little cousin, who's about five years old, always speaks carefully to me whenever we visit. He tells me: 'Grandma, you know, this is the place that Sinai was killed'. He takes my hand and brings me to a spot where he thinks is the exact place where she was killed. He stands there and tells me: 'This is the place Sinai was killed – do you remember her grandma?' I say: 'Yes, I do remember her', and we stand there quietly.

While these may sound like small things, it's as if these events happening so close to home have brought me a different awareness about many things.

You've spoken about how there have been two different sorts of understanding that have become more significantly known to you since the bombing: one involving a different knowledge of the devastating effects such losses can have on families; and another involving a renewed and different appreciation of the ways in which people gradually take steps to reclaim their lives. Can I ask you a few questions about both of those areas? I'd be very interested to know how both those areas of knowledge may have influenced your therapy, or other aspects of your life. If you have these different appreciations for the experience of families in these circumstances, what difference has this made for you ... ? Has it made a difference?

As a therapist, I think I have become more patient with both stories. I know the process takes time, and I know that there are two stories to develop. It seems as if I'm more patient to be with people in their experiences. I am more available to people to be able to share the desolation they may experience. Perhaps this is true in life in general and not only as a therapist. I certainly take more time to explore the profound effects of problems in people's lives, and I also spend more time in thoroughly creating a context for alternative, preferred stories to be described.

If someone was coming to see you, how would they experience this patience? What do you think would be different for them?

I think I have become a better listener. I wait more patiently to hear the small clues that people offer in conversations that indicate they are opening up to different ways of being, different options, different stories. Where once I might have interrupted and started asking questions, now it is generally after I have listened and heard some clues that I then start to enquire as to their meaning. I think this would make a difference to the people consulting me. It's as if I offer a little more permission for people to speak without interruption. They make the moves and then I follow-up with enquiries.

Would there be a particular person you've consulted with who you can remember listening to differently?

A young woman who was also the victim of a suicide bombing consulted me sometime ago. The bombing took place at a disco which she regularly frequented. Many of her friends, including her boyfriend, were wounded. I think my approach to the conversations we shared was influenced by the things we have been talking about. Whenever she spoke about her fears, her sadness, her loss, I didn't divert her from these losses. Instead I listened and asked about what these losses meant to her, what they represented, what she had treasured about the people who had been killed and why. At other times, she would speak about music – she wished to become reconnected with music which was a great love of her life. At these times, again, I went with her, at her own pace. I asked questions about the place of music in her history and her wishes for the future. It was gentle and patient work.

And this you think was due to the different knowledge you now have about how an experience like she had been through devastates so many aspects of life, and also a different knowledge you now have about the ways in which people take steps towards a recovery of what is precious to them?

I guess I have always known about people's wishes, hopes and skills in reclaiming their lives, because I have been a therapist for so many years. But I do think that I have a different capacity now, a different patience, to be able to speak about sadness and fear and the truly desolate places that we can find ourselves in at times in our lives.

I'm also wondering about whether there were things that you had learned over the years about being a therapist that influenced your experience of loss, or how you related to those whose lives had been devastated ...

I have had many years of hearing stories from people about how they have overcome great difficulties in their lives, and perhaps this assisted me to remain hopeful. Having the company of so many people's stories can be comforting in some way at these times. Perhaps I was attentive to double-stories (of both pain and survival) in ways that others might not be. This could have made a difference. Until now I have not thought about this. Perhaps I was open to noticing small changes, and knew that over time these could be openings to different ways of seeing the world ...

Were there any stories of others you had witnessed in the past that were particularly significant to you?

There was a friend I spoke with when she had lost her three-year-old daughter to cancer. We had spoken about loss and its meanings, and after the bombing I called her up to ask if she was willing to talk with Sinai's parents. It seemed to me that she had a whole range of experiences and insider-knowledge about responding to the death of a small child, especially as she now has a very rich and full life. She said that she was very willing to do this. Now that I think of it, yes, there were particular stories that were significant to draw upon.

I have just one other question to ask you and it is about the images that sometimes remain etched in people's memories of the moments of terror, of trauma. Are there ways in which you try as a therapist to respond to these images?

Your question reminds me of a different story, an inter-generational story. I consulted a man in therapy, called Jacob, whose father had been in Auschwitz. His father had lost three sons and his wife, who were all killed by the Nazis. He then went back to Poland where they had lived before the war. He went back to the village and all that was left was one Jewish family that had fled to Russia and then recently returned. All the other Jews of the village had perished. The family that remained were bakers and the baker told him that he could come and stay with them as long as he was happy to marry his eldest daughter. The baker had four daughters and was very afraid about what would happen to them as no other Jews were left. So, he married this young woman who was maybe 18 or 20 years old, while he was just over thirty. They moved to Israel, became farmers and, from this marriage Jacob was born.

Jacob had two sisters and was the middle child. Their father never overcame the trauma of the Holocaust. He was a very depressed man who stayed mainly in bed. The only connection Jacob had with his father was that his father would get furious with him and beat him for not working hard enough on the farm. Being the only son, the father had expectations that he would work on the farm and the relationship they had was terrible.

In time, Jacob took over the farm, got married and had four boys of his own. He came to see me in therapy after his oldest son was killed. He was a soldier on the border of Lebanon and was shot and killed. Jacob described that he had had the same sort relationship with his son as he had with his father. The only connection had been one of anger. Jacob had been angry at him for not working hard enough on the farm. And then this son was killed. Jacob came to therapy saying that, after his son was killed, many people took the time to tell him how great his boy had been. Jacob had been just sitting alone saying to himself over and over again: 'Everyone knows my boy and I don't. I didn't know him, and now he's killed and I will never know him.' This is what brought him to therapy. He still had three boys and he wanted to have a better connection with them and with his partner.

The reason I mention this story is that the most significant aspect of our therapeutic conversations together involved considerations of particular imagery. At first, all the memories that Jacob had of his father were negative. He told me many stories about these bad memories. After some time, I asked if he had any different memories of he and his father doing anything together, or just any other memories that did not consist of violence, anger and abuse. Jacob took his time to think about this and described a time when he was in boarding school. He had come home during the school holidays and he and his father walked together from the family home to the synagogue. This was a ten minute walk and, during the walk, Jacob's father took his hand. They walked hand-in-hand towards the synagogue for a few minutes. This was the only memory Jacob could recall which was a good memory.

I asked him to imagine what his father's hand would have been saying to his hand if it could have spoken during that walk to the synagogue. Jacob found this image to be very moving. And he cried when he speculated about what his father's hand would have wanted to convey at that time. He thought it might have said something like: 'Son, it's not that I don't like you, I hope you can understand what I went through. If I could, I would tell you how much you mean to me. I just cannot and it's due to what happened to me during the war.'

The first time I heard this story was when I interviewed Jacob in front of his family. We had arranged that I would interview Jacob with the rest of the family acting as outsider-witnesses. Jacob told this story about the hands and spoke about how much he wanted his relationships with his sons to be different. His partner and sons then offered their reflections. Everyone spoke. The first to do so was his youngest son who said: 'Father, we can do it, I promise, I will be close to you and you will be able to talk to me'.

This image of two hands talking has remained very significant to Jacob. One of his other sons has been going through a difficult time recently and the image of the hands is always present in their conversations. Jacob says to me now: 'I tell my son what the hand should have told me'.

I have found that many people who have suffered trauma vividly recall certain images that are associated with the trauma. For the young woman who was there when the disco place was bombed, the image she continued to see was of two cats and everything burning. The last thing that she saw before she was taken out in the ambulance were these two cats looking at the fire. Overtime, we gave these cats voices also. At first when she gave voice to their experience, they spoke with a voice of horror. But eventually this changed, and their voices began to represent continuing life. This is just one way to work with the images that are recurring in people's minds. I am sure there are many others.

In fact, Sinai's father tells a different story. He now has a scar on his face because he was also wounded in the attack. He's a very handsome man with long hair which he ties back in a ponytail, and now he has this scar. For a long time, whenever he looked in the mirror and saw these scars he would see the face of his daughter when he took her to the ambulance. This was a terrible image that kept returning to him. He has worked very deliberately to remember other images of her face, from photographs, from memory. Usually in Jewish funerals the body is covered, but Sinai's father asked to see her before she was buried. He did this to correct the image of her head, of her face. He wants to remember her as beautiful.

I think it is significant for us to inquire about the imagery that is being strongly evoked in people's lives after traumatic events. Just as we seek to create a context in which alternative story-lines can develop, I think we also need to create a context for the development of alternative imagery. In my experience, these processes often run hand-in-hand.

Thanks Yael. I've no doubt that the stories you have shared here will mean a lot to those who read them and will assist them in responding to those who have experienced severe trauma.

CHAPTER SEVEN

Children, trauma and subordinate storyline development

by Michael White

In this chapter, Michael White emphasises the importance of subordinate storyline development in consultations with children who have been subject to trauma. This subordinate storyline development provides an alternative territory of identity for children to stand in as they begin to give voice to their experiences of trauma. This affords children a significant degree of immunity from the potential for re-traumatisation in response to therapeutic initiatives to assist them to speak of their experiences of trauma and its consequences. This chapter includes illustrations of the implications of these ideas for consultations with children who have been subject to trauma.

Children are not strangers to trauma. In most societies around the globe the incidence of the abuse of children remains high despite many initiatives undertaken by state and community organisations to address this. And in most parts of the world that are experiencing the calamities associated with war, disease, displacement, and economic turmoil, children remain most acutely vulnerable to life-threatening hardship and trauma. Service providers who work in local child-protection services with the families of refugees, and those who work with people in parts of the world that are ravaged by war and disease, will be acutely aware of the importance of assisting children to recover from the effects of the trauma they have been subject to. And they will also be aware of the importance of doing this in ways that are psychologically and emotionally safe for these children who have experienced so little physical safety in the history of their young lives and, in many circumstances, when the achievement of this physical safety cannot be guaranteed.

The importance of attending to this safety is underscored by the reluctance of many children, who have been through trauma, to speak of their experience of this trauma. While there are numerous theories about this reluctance – for example, that this is due to psychological mechanisms of denial and suppression – it would seem that concerns about retribution should the trauma of abuse be disclosed, and about the potential risk of reliving trauma in the context of giving voice to this, are high on the list of relevant understandings of children's reluctance to speak of their experiences of trauma. This concern about encountering re-traumatisation upon giving expression to experiences of trauma will be a significant focus of the discussion in this paper.

I believe this concern is well-founded, for there is an ever-potential hazard that, in speaking of their experiences of trauma, children will be re-traumatised; that children will become trapped in the immediacy of their experience of the trauma they have lived through; that they will be ensnared in the reliving of this experience. This very outcome can be witnessed in circumstances in which children give voice to their experience of trauma in ways that contribute to a reinforcement of the negative conclusions they hold about their identity and about their lives. This, in turn, is usually associated with an escalation of a sense of shame, of vulnerability, of hopelessness, of desolation, and of futility. If great care is not taken in building a context in which what might be called 'psychological and emotional safety' is ascertained for the child, then there is a strong chance that the child, in response to encouragement to express their experience of trauma, will find themselves redefined by the trauma they have been subject to.

This assertion is not founded upon 'armchair' observation. Over the years I have met with many children in many contexts who have been re-traumatised through the very efforts that have been undertaken to assist them to address experiences of trauma. And on occasions I have had the excruciating experience of witnessing such re-traumatisation in process when I have not been in a position to influence the shape of the 'healing practices' being administered.

Repositioning

Attention to this aspect of psychological and emotional safety in working with children who have been subject to trauma cannot be too strongly emphasised. How can we ensure that children are not vulnerable to an experience of re-traumatisation in the context of speaking about what they have been through? This question encourages considerations of the 'psychological positioning' of the child in opening space for them to address their experiences of trauma. Another way of stating this: this question leads us to considerations of the territory of identity that the child is standing in as they go about putting expression to their experiences of abuse. If this is a territory of identity that is circumscribed by the trauma that the child has been subject to, then it can be predicted that to simply encourage the child to give expression to their experiences of this trauma will be re-traumatising, and that this will contribute to a renewed sense of vulnerability.

In addressing options for the sort of re-positioning of children that will provide a safe context for them to give expression to their experiences of trauma, narrative practices that enable the identification and rich development of the subordinate storylines of these children's lives can be employed. As these subordinate storylines are developed, they provide an alternative territory of identity for children to take recourse to in speaking of their experiences of trauma. In this chapter I will focus on options for the development of these subordinate storylines and on how these can establish territories of safety for children who have been subject to trauma.

In emphasising this focus, I don't want to be misunderstood on the subject of supporting children to speak about their experiences of trauma. It is clearly important for children to have the opportunity to speak of trauma and its consequences; to be provided with support in putting to words that which has not been spoken. I have consistently found that when children have territories of identity available to them which provide the sort of safety I have been describing, they invariably engage in powerful expressions of their experiences of trauma and its consequences. And these are expressions of the sort that provide an antidote to the sense of shame, hopelessness, desolation, and futility that is invariably reinforced in the context of re-traumatisation.

Subordinate storyline development

The genesis of subordinate storyline development[1] is to be found in children's responses to the trauma they have been subject to. No child is a passive recipient of trauma, regardless of the nature of this trauma. Amongst other things, children take action to minimise their exposure to trauma and to decrease their vulnerability to it by modifying the traumatic episodes they are subject to, or by finding ways of modifying the effects of this trauma on their lives. However, it is rare for children's responses to the traumas of their lives to be acknowledged. It is more common for these responses to go unnoticed, or to be punished, or to be disqualified through ridicule and diminishment within the trauma context.

These responses to trauma and its consequences are founded upon what children give value to; upon what they hold precious in their lives. And these responses reflect knowledges about, and skills in:

a. the preservation of life in life-threatening contexts,

b. finding support in hostile environments,

c. establishing domains of safety in unsafe places,

d. holding onto possibilities for life in circumstances that are discouraging of this,

e. developing nurturing responses to others in situations that are degrading of such responses,

f. finding connection and a sense of affiliation with others in settings that are isolating,

g. refusing to visit trauma on the lives of others in milieus that are encouraging of this reproduction of trauma,

h. healing from the consequences of trauma under conditions that are unfavourable to this,

i. achieving degrees of self-acceptance in atmospheres that are sponsoring of self-rejection,

j. and more.

These knowledges and skills are rarely independently constructed and developed by children who have been subject to trauma. Rather, it is invariably the case that these knowledges and skills have been constructed and developed in partnership with other children and with adults who are also subject to, or who have been subject to, trauma. And, further, this collaboration in the construction and development of these knowledges and skills is usually very significantly shaped by specific familial, community and cultural ethos.

In addressing this subject of children's responses to trauma, and in naming some of the knowledges and skills expressed in these responses, I am not suggesting that trauma is anything but painful for children, that it does not have highly negative consequences for the lives of children who are subject to it, or that this experience of trauma and its consequences does not need to be addressed. And I am not suggesting that for children to hold onto what they give value to, or to develop knowledges and skills of the sort to which I have referred, is enough to mitigate this pain and these consequences. My intention in drawing attention to the significance of these responses to trauma is to emphasise the fact that the negative consequences of trauma do not represent the whole story of a child's life and identity, and to give an account of some of the 'material' that is ever-available for the sort of subordinate storyline development that constructs alternative territories of identity that can be occupied by children in giving expression to their experience of trauma. These are alternative territories of identity that will make it possible for children to give expression to their experiences of trauma but not be re-traumatised in the process of doing so.

In regard to this appreciation of the fact that the negative consequences of trauma do not represent the whole story of children's lives, it can be helpful to think of memories of trauma that exclude an account of children's responses to trauma as 'half memories'. In the context of this understanding, subordinate storyline development contributes to 'full memory' restoration. I believe this 'full memory' restoration to be critically important in therapeutic consultations with children who have been subject to trauma.

Subordinate storyline development in work with children who have been subject to trauma contributes to the rich description of the child's responses to trauma, and of what these responses reflect in terms of:

1. What children give value to; of what they hold precious – which includes specific beliefs, guiding principles, hopes, dreams, personal integrities, personal ethics, and so on.

2. What children intend for their lives – which includes specific purposes, goals, ambitions, objectives, wishes, quests, pursuits, aspirations, and so on.

3. The knowledges and skills expressed in these responses – which includes the knowledges and skills associated with the points on page 147: a. through to j.

4. The social, relational and cultural genesis of these responses – which includes the contribution of significant figures in the child's history (including peers), specific family legacies that can be honoured, significant

children's literature, edifying cultural myth, ethnic traditions and concepts of spirituality, and so on.

In regard to this fourth point, as previously stated, the knowledges and skills expressed in children's responses to trauma are rarely independently constructed and developed by these children, but are developed in partnership with others, as is what children hold precious and what they intend for their lives. When the social, relational and cultural genesis of these knowledges and skills, and of what children hold precious, and of what they intend for their lives, is revealed in the context of subordinate story-line development, there are opportunities for children to experience the stories of their lives linked anew with the stories of the lives of others. Many of these others are significant figures in the child's history, and as the contribution of these figures becomes more visible, new opportunities are presented for these children to connect/reconnect with their relational/social/community networks. This can be in part facilitated by supporting children in the identification of, and in the explicit acknowledgement of, the contribution of these figures. Such acknowledgement can take many forms, including in the form of letters and certificates of recognition co-developed/co-written by children and their counsellors/community workers, and in the form of honouring ceremonies for these figures planned by children in collaboration with these counsellors/ community workers.

The accounts of what children hold precious, and of what they intend for their lives that are featured in subordinate storyline development can be thought of as concepts about life and about identity. The extent to which children have formed these concepts is dependent upon the stage and state of the child's development, and even for older children these concepts are rarely fully formed. In consultations that contribute to subordinate storyline development for children, these concepts are not usually 'discovered' completely formed, but are further developed in the context of therapeutic conversations in which the counsellor/community worker is a conversational partner. It is my understanding that such conceptual development is critical to the establishment of children's ability to intervene in shaping their own lives and of their ability to influence their relationships with others (Vygotsky 1986).

I have reiterated the point that, in rendering more visible the sources of children's responses to trauma, subordinate storyline development provides a safe place for children to stand in the context of giving voice to the trauma they have been subject to, and to the consequences of this trauma. But this is not all. This subordinate storyline development also provides a foundation for action for children to proceed with their lives. As these subordinate storylines become more richly known and experienced, it becomes more possible for children to take initiatives that are in harmony with what they give value to, with what they intend for their lives, and that are shaped by the knowledges and skills that are of their own histories. It also becomes more possible for them to further develop their connections with those who are significant to them, and with valued aspects of culture and history.

In focussing on the subject of subordinate storyline development in this paper, there is a risk that I will be understood to be suggesting that the conversations of narrative therapy are revealing of an alternative story that is the 'true' or 'authentic' story. However, this is not the case. To the contrary, I understand life to be multi-storied, and all of the alternative stories of life to be cultural, relational and historical in origin; these stories are all possible constructions of the events and experiences of life. And in subordinate storyline development, I am aware that there are often opportunities for people to experience being positioned simultaneously in more than one field of existence, in more than one territory of identity.

Personal agency

In rendering more visible children's responses to trauma according to the terms that I have defined here, subordinate storyline development restores children's sense of personal agency. This is a sense of self that is associated with the perception that one is able to have some effect on the shape of one's own life; a sense that one is able to intervene in one's own life as an agent of what one gives value to and as an agent of one's own intentions, and a sense that the world is at least minimally responsive to the fact of one's existence.

The restoration and/or development of this sense of personal agency in work with children who have been subject to trauma is of critical importance. The restoration and/or development of this sense of personal agency provides an antidote to the sort of highly disabling conclusions about one's identity that feature perceptions that one is a passive recipient of life's forces. Such perceptions are highly influential in the development of conclusions that one is 'damaged' and 'messed up' on account of what one has been through, and to the development of the pervasive and profoundly immobilising phenomena of 'vulnerability' and 'fragility'.

The contribution that subordinate storyline development might make as an antidote to these negative identity conclusions that children have often derived is of critical importance, particularly in these contemporary times in which the discourses of victimhood have become so influential in the construction of the identities of people who have been subject to trauma. These discourses have become prominent in the professional and the popular psychologies, and not only promote the construction of disabled identities, but also shape relationship practices that are diminishing and marginalising of people who have been through significant trauma. In the context of these relationship practices, people who have been subject to significant trauma become the 'other'. It is in the context of these relationship practices that their identity is constructed as 'spoiled'.

In regard to service provision, when workers are encouraged to place their sole focus on the trauma that children have been subject to, and on the consequences of this trauma, they become vulnerable to the reproduction of these discourses of victimhood in their therapeutic work. In this circumstance, there is a risk that counsellors/community workers will further diminish children's sense of personal agency and, as well, inadvertently reinforce a passive-recipient identity status for these children. This central and exclusive focus on trauma and its consequences obscures the extent to which identity is constructed in language and in the context of relational practices. And it obscures the extent to which it is identity that is very much at stake in work with children who have been subject to abuse.

This is an important matter, for the contemporary discourses of victimhood have serious consequences for child development, and can contribute very significantly to the long-term establishment of a sense of 'emptiness' and 'desolation' in life. These contemporary discourses of victimhood also have serious consequences for the therapeutic relationship in work with children. Although many therapists/community workers have an awareness of the conditions that can contribute to the development of 'learned helplessness' in the people who seek their help, this term is far too mild a description of the potential devastation that these discourses of victimhood can wreak in young people's lives.

I believe that the modern and popular interpretation of the concept of catharsis has played a significant role in obscuring the play of these discourses of victimhood. This interpretation of this concept is associated with the idea that human action is founded upon an emotional/psychological system that works according to the principles of hydraulic and steam-engine technology; for example, that emotions are held under pressure within this system like a head of steam is held under pressure in a steam engine, and that the 'discharge' or 'release' of this pressure through the appropriate 'valve' will culminate in the desired outcome. According to this concept, the pain of trauma is held under pressure in the emotional/psychological system, and the discharge of this pain via an appropriate avenue will be a panacea in regard to the effects of this trauma. Under the sway of this interpretation of the concept of catharsis, counsellors often encourage people to give expression to their experiences of trauma without engaging with considerations about the safety of doing so; without a foundation for contemplating the potential for this to be re-traumatising for people, for understanding how this might be constructing of people's identity, and without a foundation for grasping the critical importance of the resurrection and/or development of a sense of personal agency for the people who are consulting them.

Identification of children's responses to trauma

I have referred to the part that the rich description of children's responses to trauma can play in subordinate storyline development, with specific reference to:

a. what children give value to,

b. what children intend for their lives,

c. the knowledges and skills expressed in these responses, and to

d. the social, relational and cultural genesis of these responses.

This begs the question: 'How can these responses be identified?' There are many avenues of therapeutic inquiry that render visible and richly describe children's responses to trauma. I will now draw out three of these avenues of therapeutic inquiry:

• identifying the absent but implicit,

• reflecting on problem-solving activity, and

• direct observation of spontaneous interaction.

I will also provide descriptions of therapeutic consultations with children which are based on each of these avenues of inquiry.

Identifying the absent but implicit

The notion of the 'absent but implicit' is associated with the idea that, in order to express one's experiences of life, one must distinguish this experience from what it is not. By this account, every expression can be considered to be founded upon its contrast, which I refer to as the 'absent but implicit'. I have drawn significantly from the work of Jaques Derrida (1973, 1976, 1978) in this understanding, which I have discussed at some length elsewhere (White 2000, 2003). For many years I have found this notion to be of service in the genesis of the subordinate storylines of people's lives. Amongst other possibilities, the notion of the absent but implicit provides opportunities for ongoing psychological pain in response to trauma to be considered a testimony to the significance of what it was that the person held precious that was violated through the experience of trauma. (See box: 'The Absent but Implicit' on the following page)

The Absent but Implicit

To clarify the implications of this understanding, I will here reproduce part of a discussion from 'Narrative Practice and Community Assignments' (White 2003, pp.39-43). This discussion presents alternative perspectives on psychological pain and emotional distress that are derived from the notion of the 'absent but implicit'.

Pain as testimony

Ongoing psychological pain in response to trauma in the history of people's lives might be considered a testimony to the significance of what it was that the person held precious that was violated through the experience of trauma. This can include people's understandings about:

a. cherished purposes for one's life;

b. prized values and beliefs around acceptance, justice and fairness;

c. treasured aspirations, hopes and dreams;

d. moral visions about how things might be in the world;

e. significant pledges, vows and commitments about ways of being in life; etc.

If psychological pain can be considered to be a testimony to such purposes, values, beliefs, aspirations, hopes, dreams, moral visions, and commitments, then the experienced intensity of this pain can be considered to be a reflection of the degree to which these intentional states were held precious by persons. In the context of therapeutic conversations, these intentional state understandings can be identified, resurrected and become richly known. As well, it is within these conversations that people have the opportunity to experience being at one with a range of positive identity conclusions that displace many negative 'truths' of identity that they have been recruited into as an outcome of the traumas they have been subject to.

Distress as tribute

Day-to-day emotional distress in response to trauma in people's histories might be considered a tribute to their ability to maintain a constant relationship with all of those purposes, values, beliefs, aspirations, hopes, dreams, visions and commitments held precious – to their refusal to relinquish or to be separated from what that was so powerfully disrespected and demeaned in the context of trauma, from what it was that they continue to revere.

If such emotional distress can be considered to be a tribute to people's determination to maintain a constant relationship with that which was powerfully disrespected and demeaned in the context of trauma, then the experienced intensity of this distress can be considered to be a reflection of the degree to which the person has continued to revere and maintain a relationship with what it is that they hold precious. In the context of therapeutic conversations, acknowledgement of people's refusal to relinquish what was so powerfully disrespected, and explorations of their skills in maintaining a relationship with these intentional states, can be very significantly elevating of their sense of who they are, and of what their lives are about.

Pain and Distress as Proclamation of response

If ongoing psychological pain can be considered a testimony to the significance of what it was that the person held precious that was violated through the experience of trauma, and if emotional distress can be considered a tribute to their ability to maintain a constant relationship with what was so powerfully disrespected and demeaned in the context of trauma, exploring the specifics of this testimony and tribute can provide a basis for identifying people's responses to the trauma they have been subject to. People respond to the crises of their lives, even when these crises are the outcome of trauma under circumstances in which they are relatively powerless to escape the context or to bring about a cessation of whatever it is that they are being subject to. Even small children who are being subject to abuse respond in ways to modify what it is that they are being subject to. These acts of redress that are shaped by people's intentional states are rarely recognised and acknowledged, and therefore rarely appreciated by and held with reverence by the people who initiate them.

When the specifics of what psychological pain and emotional distress might be a testimony or tribute to are defined, this can provide a basis for explorations of the extent to which this pain and distress is also a proclamation of people's responses to the traumas that they have been subject to. In the context of therapeutic conversations, what it is that a person held precious and has continued to revere can become known, and this provides the basis for an inquiry into how this shaped their responses to what they were being put through. This sort of inquiry is one that emphasises actions taken that reflect the exercise of personal agency according to specific intentional states.

Psychological pain and distress as elements of a legacy

Psychological pain and emotional distress might be understood to be elements of a legacy expressed by people who, in the face of the non-responsiveness of the world around them, remain resolute in their determination that the trauma that they and others have gone through will not be for nothing – that things must change on account of what they have gone through. According to this understanding, despite the absence of a wider acknowledgement that things must change, these people are sentinels who will not let this matter drop, and who have remained on guard against forces that would be diminishing of their experiences, and that would be reproducing of trauma in the lives of others.

This understanding contributes to a context in which the legacy that is represented in expressions of psychological pain and emotional distress can be significantly honoured and joined with by others. It can also contribute to a context that is acknowledging of the way in which people rely upon their insider experience of trauma in recognising the consequences of this in the lives of others, and in responding to others with a compassion that touches their lives, and that evokes a sense of solidarity with them.

Deanne

Deanne, ten years of age, had been referred to me with an explicit request that I assist her to express her experiences of very significant trauma that she'd been subject to. Various efforts to achieve this had already been undertaken in three different counselling contexts, but the outcome of these efforts had been largely negative. In response to these efforts, Deanne had become highly distressed, then regressed and, following each instance, had felt quite unstable for a period of weeks.

At the outset of my meetings with Deanne I made it clear that I had no expectations in regard to her speaking about the trauma that she'd been put through, but enquired as to whether it would be okay to ask her a few questions about the distress that she'd been managing. This was okay by Deanne, so I initiated an inquiry into what it might be that was precious to her that had been hurt by the abuse she'd experienced, suggesting that the intensity of this distress might correspond with the strength to which she held whatever it was precious in her life; with perhaps the degree of passion that she felt for what she gave value to in her life. In response to these questions, Deanne began to talk about her sense of the unfairness of what she'd been through, and this led to a conversation about specific principles of fairness that had always been important to her. Before long I was hearing stories about some of the initiatives of Deanne's life that were a reflection of these principles, including one about action that she'd recently been taking in solidarity with another girl at school who'd also been through hard times and who was the subject of peer abuse.

In our second meeting, amongst other things, we embarked upon explorations of the history of these principles of fairness in Deanne's life. It was in these explorations that Deanne for the first time established a link between her voice on these principles of fairness, and one of her favourite books – Pippi Longstocking (Lindgren 1950). In our third meeting we did some shared reading of the passages of Pippi Longstocking that Deanne was most drawn to, and in which these principles were expressed. This meeting culminated with me assisting Deanne to write a letter to Astrid Lingren, Pippi Longstocking's creator, which acknowledged this author's contribution to Deanne's sense of fairness. Deanne clearly experienced joy in this task.

For our fourth meeting, with Deanne's approval, I invited some other young people to join as outsider witnesses[2]. These were young people who'd consulted me about trauma in the past, and who'd volunteered to join me in my work with other young people who might be following in their footsteps. The powerfully resonant re-tellings of Deanne's story by these outsider witnesses had a very positive effect on Deanne's conclusions about her own identity.

In our fifth meeting, at which these outsider witnesses were again present, I found opportunity to consult Deanne about her thoughts on whether her principles of fairness had played a role in her survival of the trauma that she'd been through. Her response was in the affirmative, and led to a conversation about the ways in which these principles had shaped her responses to this trauma. As these responses were drawn out Deanne began to speak openly of the specific details of this trauma and, although this was an emotional time for her, there was not a hint that she was encountering any re-traumatisation or regression as an outcome of this. Again, the re-tellings of the outsider witnesses were powerfully resonant for Deanne – this time the focus of these re-tellings was placed on Deanne's experience of trauma, its consequences, and on her response to this.

At our sixth meeting I learned that Deanne had not experienced any destabilising effects from giving such direct expression to her experience of abuse. Rather, she experienced her life proceeding in unexpectedly positive ways. This emboldened her to put more words to what she'd previously been unable to speak of and, as one outcome of so doing, Deanne found that this didn't upset her in the way that she'd predicted it would. To Deanne, this was, of itself, a valued learning, and a significantly positive reflection on her personal development.

Upon reviewing, with Deanne, the contribution of the re-tellings of outsider witnesses, it became quite clear that these had played a highly significant role in the acknowledgement of the trauma, its consequences, and of Deanne's response to this trauma. It also became quite clear that these re-tellings played a significant role in the restoration of and further development of her sense of personal agency.

Reflecting on problem-solving activity

Problem-solving activity can provide a fertile context for rendering visible what it is that children give value to, what they intend for their lives, and the knowledges of life and skills of living that are important to them. In witnessing children engaging in such activity, counsellors/community workers can note children's responses to the task to be solved and their responses to each other as they go about addressing the task. Following this, these children can be interviewed about these responses, and about their further reflections on the experience of the problem-solving activity.

Imbrahim, Amir, and Alex

I was meeting with Imbrahim, Amir, and Alex, who had migrated from their countries of origin as refugees. They had been referred to me on account of concerns about their generally withdrawn status, and about the extent to which they had continued to maintain silence in regard to the very significant trauma that they had been subject to over an extended period ahead of their migration.

We'd taken a walk together in a nearby park. On account of a recent storm, the small creek in this park had been turned into a torrent. The three boys determined that this would have to be traversed, and set about figuring out how this might be done – the creek was not deep and could not have swept them away, but there was a very real risk that they could have fallen in and become wet through. With the aid of various props that they found in the park, in a spirit of challenge and adventure, and with each other's support, eventually all three had succeeded in crossing to and fro without getting wet.

Afterwards we sat and talked about what had gone into the task that had ensured its success. Imbrahim, Amir and Alex's reflections on this, along with their verbal utterances that had accompanied the adventure itself, provided me with a foundation to interview them about what they held precious, and about their intentional understandings of their actions. I will include here a small sample of the sort of questions that shaped this interview:

Questions of Imbrahim

Imbrahim, you said that at one point you'd been scared for Alex, more scared for him than you'd been for yourself. And you also said that this was about 'looking out for others'.

- What did this 'looking out for others' make possible for you in the creek adventure?
- What is your guess about what this did for Amir and Alex?
- How did you feel about making this contribution?
- What does this say about what is important to you?
- Can you tell me some other stories of your life that reflect this ability to 'look out for others'?

Questions of Amir

Amir, I heard you say something about how at one point you worried that it couldn't be done, but that you kept on because you knew how good it would feel when you did get to the other side.

- What is a good name for how you keep trying to get to the other side when things are difficult or scary?

- How did this play a part in the creek adventure working out like it did?

- How did you feel about playing this part?

- I understand that it was about 'keeping on trying' and 'knowing that things will be better' when you get to the other side. Would you say something about what you have learned in your life about getting through things that are difficult?

- Can you tell me some stories about your life that reflect these learnings about getting through things that are difficult?

Questions of Alex

Alex, you said that you set a goal for yourself, and that you were not going to give up on this goal, no matter what. What is a good name for this capacity to hold onto goals that are important to you, and to see these through?

- How did this affect what you did in the creek adventure?

- What was it like for you to find yourself holding onto this goal in the way that you did?

- What does this say about what you want for your life?

- Can you tell me some stories about your life that are examples of you refusing to let go of your goals, and that are examples of standing for what you want in life?

I had several more meetings with Imbrahim, Amir, and Alex, and these provided the opportunity for me to enquire into the relational/social/cultural histories of what these young men held precious, of their intentional understandings of their actions, and of the knowledges and skills that were richly described in our conversations. One outcome of the conversations that were generated by this line of inquiry was that Imbrahim, Amir, and Alex realised that the stories of their lives were linked to valued stories of their cultural history in ways that they could rejoice in.

When I sensed that subordinate storyline development was such that it afforded alternative and relatively secure territories of identity for these young men to occupy, I began to consult them about whether what they held precious and what they intended for their lives, along with these various capacities, knowledges and skills, had played part in them getting through the trauma they'd experienced. The response was a unanimous 'yes'. In the context of providing an account of this, these three young men gave vivid detail to their experiences of trauma. I encouraged them to reflect on what it was like for them to be giving voice to the hard things they'd been through, and learned that this was the first time that they'd been able to speak of this without feeling 'absolutely terrible' afterward.

My latter meetings with Imbrahim, Amir, and Alex were structured around outsider-witness practices. In these meetings they took turns for each other in the development of re-tellings of the trauma they'd each been through, of the consequences of this, and of their responses to this trauma. These re-tellings were highly significant in the acknowledgement of the trauma and its consequences, and of their responses to this trauma. And, as with Deanne, for each boy these re-tellings played a significant role in the restoration and further development of their sense of personal agency.

Direct observation of spontaneous interaction

Direct observation of the spontaneous interaction of children who have been subject to trauma can provide clues about points of entry for subordinate storyline development.

James, Emily and Beth

In my first meeting with James (11 years), Emily (8 years), and Beth (7 years), siblings who had been through very significant abuse and neglect in their young lives, on several occasions I witnessed James engaging in the care-taking of his sisters. This care-taking was evident in several ways, including in the patience that he expressed in assisting Emily and Beth to clarify what they thought about some relatively simple subjects that I consulted them about.

This observation provided a foundation for a therapeutic inquiry in which, amongst other things, I encouraged James, Emily and Beth to:

a. name these care-taking skills,

b. describe the know-how that was expressed in these skills,

c. define the contribution of these skills to Emily's life and Beth's life,

d. speculate about what the possession of these skills might make possible for James in the future of his own life,

e. reflect on what these skills might say about what is most important to James,

f. trace the history of the development of these skills in James' life, and to

g. identify figures of James' history who might have valued and appreciated these skills, and who might be implicated in his development of these skills.

As it turned out that James' teacher from his third grade was a figure who was implicated in the development of his care-taking skills, she was invited to our third, fourth, and fifth meetings. In the role of outsider witness, this teacher played a very significant part in the rich development of a sub-ordinate storyline of James' life, in the acknowledgement of the trauma that James (as well as Emily and Beth) had been subject to, and in the restoration and further development of his sense of personal agency.

Emily's and Beth's responsiveness to James' care-taking did not go unnoticed. This provided the foundation for explorations that were focussed on how they had been able to open themselves to the concern and support of others, and on their skills in connecting with others.

When the time seemed right, I began to enquire about whether these skills had had a part to play in providing a foundation for these children to get through the hard times they'd experienced. At this point, all three children became quite animated in giving accounts of how they had used these skills to survive the abuse and neglect that had been visited upon them. These were dramatic and vivid accounts, which included specific details of what they had been subject to, which they had mostly never previously spoken of. Over several more meetings it was clear that James, Emily and Beth now had a foundation for giving voice to their experiences of abuse and neglect in ways that were not accompanied by a risk that they would be defined by this abuse and neglect, in ways that were not accompanied by a risk that they could be re-traumatised in this.

Conclusion

In this paper, I have emphasised the importance of subordinate storyline development in consultations with children who have been subject to trauma. This subordinate storyline development provides an alternative territory of identity for children to stand in as they begin to give voice to their experiences of trauma. This affords children a significant degree of immunity from the potential for re-traumatisation in response to therapeutic initiatives to assist them to speak of their experiences of trauma and its consequences. I have also provided some illustrations of the implications of these ideas for consultations with children who have been subject to trauma. In a future paper on this subject I intend to illustrate the relevance of these considerations to younger children.

In emphasising these considerations of safety, it is not my intention to sponsor avoidance, on behalf of counsellors and community workers, of the facts of the trauma that children have been subject to. And in my own work with people who have been subject to trauma, I have not sought to attenuate their expressions of trauma and its consequences. I have not been timid in opening space for people to speak of what they have not had the opportunity to speak of, to put words to what has been unmentionable. This has been so for my meetings with people who have been subject to a range of abuses, including political torture, and for people struggling with trauma that is the outcome of a range of social calamities, including disease epidemics. However, I have taken care to do what is within my understandings and skills to establish contexts in which people can give full voice to their experiences of trauma in ways that enable them to wrest their lives from the prospective longer term consequences of this trauma. And I have never accepted that any person need be re-traumatised in the context of assisting them to address what they have been through.

Notes

1. I will refer to 'subordinate storyline' development when describing the further development of some of the alternative stories of children's lives that are to be found in thin traces, in the shadows of the dominant stories of their lives. This description seems apt, as it is not by chance that these storylines are relatively invisible at the outset of therapeutic conversations. These storylines have been subordinated in the context of the politics of disqualification, diminishment, ridicule and marginalisation.

2. Outsider-witness participation is a regular feature of my consultations. For an account of the scaffolding of outsider-witness participation in therapeutic practice, and of the tradition of acknowledgement that shapes the re-tellings of outsider witnesses, see White 2004a & 2004b.

References

Derrida, J. 1973: *Speech and Phenomena, and other Essays on Husserl's Theory of Signs.* Evanston: Northwestern University Press.

Derrida, J. 1976: *Of Grammatology.* Baltimore: John Hopkins University Press.

Derrida, J. 1978: *Writing and Difference.* London: Routledge and Kegan Paul.

Lindgren, A. 1950: *Pippi Longstocking.* New York: Viking Press

Vygotsky, L. 1986: *Thought and Language.* Cambridge, Massachusetts: The MIT Press.

White, M. 2000: 'Re-engaging with history: The absent but implicit.' In White, M.: *Reflections on Narrative Practice: Essays & interviews* (chapter 3), pp.35-58. Adelaide: Dulwich Centre Publications.

White, M. 2003: 'Narrative practice and community assignments.' *International Journal of Narrative Therapy and Community Work,* 2:17-55.

White, M. 2004a: 'Narrative practice, couple therapy and conflict dissolution.' In White, M.: *Narrative Practice & Exotic Lives: Resurrecting diversity in everyday life* (chapter 1), pp.1-41. Adelaide: Dulwich Centre Publications.

White, M. 2004b: 'Working with people who are suffering the consequences of multiple trauma: a narrative perspective.' *The International Journal of Narrative Therapy and Community Work,* 1:47-76.

CHAPTER EIGHT

Glimpses of therapeutic
conversations:

engaging with narrative ideas

by Bilal Hassounh, Iman Ja'ouni,

Deema Al Tibi, Amani Al-Jamal,

Maryam Burqan, Wisam Abdallah

This chapter consists of short descriptions of work by practitioners from the Treatment and Rehabilitation Centre for Victims of Torture (TRC) which is based in Ramallah, in the occupied Palestinian Territories. This organisation was founded by Dr Mahmud Sehwail and provides counselling, psychological and psychiatric services to the Palestinian community. When trying to respond to experiences of trauma in the context of occupation, when the trauma people are experiencing is not past or post, but is continuing, how can workers respond? In recent years the TRC has become interested in narrative ideas. In this chapter, a number of workers describe how they have been putting narrative practices to work in their context.

From sadness to song
By Bilal Hassounh

Sharaf is a twenty-eight-year-old man who came to our TRC offices in Hebron suffering from the effects of trauma and schizophrenia. Sharaf had developed schizophrenia after the first time he was arrested and this meant his second incarceration was a terrible experience. He had no treatment or medication while he was in prison. He was interrogated and left in a small cell alone for fourteen days. The lighting in the cell was bad and during this time the voices and delusions became very strong. He sought treatment when he was released and was placed on medication. This medication, however, did not help him and in some ways the illness became worse. Sharaf came to us after he had been released from his third time in prison. He was seen by our doctor who changed the medication, and my role was to support him through therapeutic conversations.

The new medication took some time to reduce the strength of the voices and delusions and we began to have some significant conversations. When I received some intensive training in narrative therapy, I became interested in whether these ideas would be helpful in our consultations. I asked Sharaf whether he would be happy for me to try out some of these ideas which were new to me. And he said he was very happy for me to do so.

As we were talking I came to see that the difficulties in Sharaf's life had become internalised. He saw himself as a depressed person, as a sad person, someone without hope. By asking some questions in an externalising way[1], slowly, slowly this changed. Over time, Sharaf began to talk about The Sadness that had come to rule his life. He could see that the main problem he was facing at present was the extent and influence of The Sadness.

When we explored the history of The Sadness, I learnt that Sharaf had once been an Islamic singer. And when he was singing, The Sadness was not present. As we began to explore what singing meant to Sharaf and its history in his life, his body language changed, his eyes lit up. Happiness was clearly present with us in the room.

I became interested in asking about Sharaf's hopes, dreams, goals and commitments, and I heard about his plans to become reconnected with singing and song. After two of these conversations he said he needed to start singing again. His first step was to travel to Ramallah to go to a centre he knew where they taught singing, and where he knew he could make connections with other musicians. His second step was to go and sing again at a restaurant in Ramallah. When he came back to Hebron after this trip he was very happy.

Sharaf then decided to hold a party for his close friends and give a concert. This was the first time for many years that he had done such a thing. He learnt new instruments and songs for the event and it was a powerfully healing ritual for him.

During this period, we also explored other times in his life when The Sadness was not so present, times when he was having other experiences of life. He began to develop a range of strategies that he could use to help himself. These included swimming, dancing, doing long walks in open spaces, reading books and practicing yoga.

In time, Sharaf spoke about how the effects of his own trauma had got in the way of him being able to assist others. He had regretted this and, as his life became more under his control rather than controlled by The Sadness, he decided that he wanted to do more for others. An opportunity arose when he was approached by some people who were struggling and who needed money. While Sharaf did not have any money to give them, he has friendships with some successful business people and decided that he could approach them. When he spoke with his friends they agreed to give a donation to this group who were desperate, and in this way Sharaf was able to make a contribution.

If I had invited Sharaf to talk more directly about his experiences of trauma, I suspect that he would have become more depressed. It would have made him more vulnerable to The Sadness and the delusions. Externalising The Sadness, however, and then seeking openings to preferred stories, seems to have enabled Sharaf to talk about aspects of his life that otherwise had become obscured. Reconnecting with preferred stories of identity related to 'singing' and 'helping others' has made a significant difference to his life.

Noticing contributions
By Amani Al-Jamal

For some time I have been working with a mother of three children, all of whom have significant disabilities. They cannot hear or speak and this mother has felt considerable sorrow and self-blame about this. She has compared her children negatively to those of other mothers, and felt overwhelmed by the misfortune that has come upon her and her family. When other people have approached her, they convey their sympathy to her about her situation and this has made her feel worse. She has felt poor and small and as if she had nothing to contribute to the world. At first, in my conversations with this mother, I was showing my empathy and trying to calm her down, but this did not seem to be making a difference. At times I was also trying to find some positive things for the mother to acknowledge, but the ways I was doing this were not resonating for her.

One day though, this mother was particularly upset – she was crying and feeling considerable despair and I noticed that her children were comforting her. They were soothing her tears, and were successfully calming her. I began to ask the mother about this and learned that this happened quite regularly. Her children were quite skilled at knowing when she was upset and how to respond to her. I also learned that, whenever foreigners came to their village, her children would show them the way to wherever they needed to go. Similarly, her older child would often assist older people around the village, and would care for other children in the special school which they attended.

These were all sparkling moments and we began to explore some of the alternative, preferred stories of these children's lives. We began to explore what seemed important to these children, what they valued and how they demonstrated this in their lives. As we made these explorations together, this mother started to notice and mention more of the contributions that these children were making. She could even recognise that she shared some of the same values and hopes for life. We did not diminish the hardships that this mother faces in her daily life, but acknowledging the contributions of the children has resulted in her feeling more optimistic.

Re-engaging with history
By Iman Ja'ouni

A forty-year-old woman from Jericho with whom I work has been struggling with serious depression since she was diagnosed with cancer. After having been through many difficulties in her life, this seemed to her to be the last straw. She was refusing to take her medication and it looked like she had given up on life. I had tried various approaches to conversations before I realised that perhaps within her own life history there might be stories and experiences that could assist her at this time. I became curious about other times in her life when she may have felt hopeless, or up against a very powerful foe. I suspected that this might not have been the first time that she had needed to face very difficult circumstances. She then began to tell me a story of when she once was in a similar situation, facing death, also from cancer. Nine years ago she had been diagnosed for the first time and she had feared for her life. I wanted to know about the difficulties she faced then, about the hardest things, the times when all had seemed hopeless. I then asked questions to learn about the skills and knowledge she had used during those most difficult times, about what had sustained her, about what she had learned, about who else had made contributions, about what she had dreamt about, how she had kept hopes alive. As we talked, she said that she had forgotten all about those times. She had become disconnected from her own skills and in the process had become disconnected from hope. In remembering some of the stories of her own life, in re-engaging with her own history, this reconnected her with hope.

Responding to grief
By Iman Ja'ouni

When working with families who have experienced grief and loss, I have become very interested in 'double-listening'[2], listening not only for stories of sorrow and distress, but also for openings to other stories, stories that convey what is important to the person, their values and beliefs. I was recently working with a mother who had lost her child in a car accident. Since her child's death she had become very depressed. It was as if a sense of hopelessness had descended upon her. When this mother spoke to me, she would say that she no longer did anything, no longer had any hopes for the future. While acknowledging the devastating effects of this accident and her child's death on her life, I was also interested to ask questions about what this mother was doing in her daily life. In asking about this, I heard that each day she was taking a range of actions, a number of which involved distributing money and assisting other families who were going through hard times. We spoke at some length about why it was important to her to assist others. When she saw other families who were struggling to care for their children, she wanted to reach out and assist in any way that she could. She missed her own child so much that she wanted to make any contribution she could to other families and children. In talking about this, we learned that these acts of care for other families were a form of commemoration or remembrance of the child she had lost.

As this alternative story developed, one that acknowledged the ways that this mother was remembering and commemorating her child, she began to speak less about the trauma. When we had first met, she would tell and re-tell the story of the accident and the loss. Now this is no longer the case. The actions she is taking in life now have become linked to honouring her child's life and this seems to have made a difference.

Re-authoring conversations with children
By Deema Al Tibi

In working with children, I have found re-authoring conversations very relevant[3]. This has been especially so in my work with an eight-year-old Palestinian boy who recently migrated to Ramallah from the USA. Being a new arrival in this country, he had been finding the adjustment very difficult. He had been stealing from others and had come to view himself and others in his family in a very negative light. His story of identity had become problematic. In fact, it had become rare to hear him speak positively about any aspect of his life.

Rather than focus the conversations only on the difficulties in this child's life, I started to become curious about the things that he values and what his hopes might be for his future. Having learned that what were most precious to him were his relationships with his family, friends and brothers and sisters, I then tried to weave conversations back and forth through his history. I was interested to know of actions that he had taken in the past that demonstrated this care for his brothers and sisters and I came to hear some stories of times that they had shared together. Gradually, I also came to hear how his preferred values were being put to use in his school.

I have found this idea of tracing the history of people's values very helpful. I have also appreciated the idea of moving between the landscape of action and the landscape of meaning[4]. These ideas have provided the opportunity to re-author stories of identity, to locate and trace the history of more helpful stories that can provide a basis for different sorts of action.

The death of a child
By Wisam Abdallah

Much of my work involves speaking with bereaved mothers who are trying to come to terms with the deaths of their children. This can be particularly difficult if the child's death has resulted from violence and injustice. I was recently working with a forty-year-old woman whose four-year-old child had been shot and killed by Israeli soldiers. To make matters even more difficult for this woman, she had not been able to see the child prior to the funeral. When children are killed in these sorts of situations, the community organises a martyr's funeral. These are very large events involving thousands of people. In this case, the mother had been unable to see her child and was finding it very difficult to come to terms with the fact that he had died. Her brother-in-law was involved in the therapy to explain everything he had seen. He had taken the child to the burial and had a video recording of the event. For the mother, being told of the events and finally realising for certain that her child had been killed was devastating. She felt as if her life was also finished. She believed that she too must die; that there was nothing left for her; nothing she could do; nothing of worth. Life had lost all meaning. To be with her was at times overwhelming. Her grief and loss were so powerful. Because she had not been able to be connected to her son in death, she also felt very isolated in the whole experience.

For a time, this mother found it very difficult to remain in her family home. The memories of her child who had been killed were so overwhelming that she needed to escape from the house, to visit her friends, who offered company and kindness

Gradually, I began to ask questions within the landscape of action. I wanted to know what occurred throughout each day. While she was telling me that there was nothing left for her to do, I learnt that she was still taking her other child to school and that she was still doing the cooking for the family. I asked her about this. I asked about what it meant that she was still prioritising these particular actions and how she was able to do this despite the devastation of her losses. These were explorations in the landscape of meaning. I asked what these actions indicated to her about what she values in life. I tried to ask about the history of these values.

In time, when the significance of her loss was acknowledged, and when her actions of care towards her still living children were honoured, she found it easier to reconnect with her family. She still feels the loss of her child very strongly, but she is no longer alone in this. She has been reunited with her family, and her friends remain significant supports.

Re-membering
By Maryam Burqan

I was recently working with a woman whose husband died five years ago. She was living alone with her nine-year-old daughter and was having some troubles in relation to her husband's family. They wanted her to move in with them. They believed her daughter should be raised by her husband's family rather than her alone. Our conversations focused on the ways in which she was keeping her husband's presence alive in her life. Through asking her a range of questions I learnt that her husband's clothes and pictures were all arranged within her family home in ways to preserve his memory. His favourite belt was hung in a particular place where she could see it from her bed. She told me: 'My husband is inside me now. He is in our home. He is here.' She described that when other difficulties in her life were strong, she could still confide in her husband.

I was interested in asking questions according to the re-membering conversations map[5], to gather richer descriptions about the contributions that the husband had made to her life, and the contributions that she had made to his life. I wanted to hear about a two-way account of this relationship as I thought this would assist to sustain her during these difficult times.

I heard that he had been a very understanding husband. Whenever there were difficult situations, he would comfort her. He encouraged her initiatives and he was very tender towards her in all aspects of life.

I then asked her about the contributions she made to her husband's life. She spoke about how she would wash his clothes, cook for him and take care of the house. She also described how she would talk to him about love, and helped him to understand many things about relationships. She knew that his life with her had been a beautiful life, that he had been very happy with her.

Honouring this two-way relationship was significant to her. She described that she thought he was in another world now, one in which he looked down at her, and saw her remembering him. She said that this made him happy and, in turn, this was significant to her.

Notes

1. For more information about externalising conversations see White, M. & Epston D. 1990: *Narrative Means to Therapeutic Ends*. New York: W. W. Norton.

2. For explanations of the importance of double listening in response to trauma see chapter 2 of this book by Michael White: 'Working with people who are suffering the consequences of multiple trauma: A narrative perspective.'

3. For more information about re-authoring conversations see Russell, S. & Carey, M. (compiled by) 2004: *Narrative Therapy: Responding to your questions*. Adelaide: Dulwich Centre Publications.

4. The stories of our lives consist of two landscapes: the landscape of action in which events take place, and the landscape of meaning (or landscape of consciousness) in which interpretations of these events are made. For more information see White, M. 1995: 'The Narrative Perspective in Therapy.' In *Re-Authoring Lives: Interviews and Essays*. Adelaide: Dulwich Centre Publications.

5. For more information about the re-membering conversations map see Michael White's Current Workshop Notes on *www.dulwichcentre.com.au*

CHAPTER NINE

The values of this work:

supporting workers' experience at the Acid Survivors Foundation

by Shona Russell, Monira Rahman, Margaret Ryan
& the workers of the Acid Survivors Foundation

This chapter describes a meeting of workers that recently took place at the Acid Survivors Foundation, in Dhaka, Bangladesh. This meeting was structured according to narrative ideas in order to explore ways of dealing with the psychological consequences of working with survivors of acid violence; to provide staff with an opportunity to speak about what is important for them in their work; to explore ways in which staff are already responding to the impact of the work on them and to consider some new possibilities. A document is included outlining the skills, knowledge, experience and values of workers at the Acid Survivors Foundation.

The Acid Survivors Foundation[1] is based in Dhaka, Bangladesh, and provides assistance to survivors of acid violence. Bangladesh has the highest world-wide incidence of acid violence. This form of violence is particularly vicious and damaging wherein acid is thrown on people's faces to destroy the beauty of a person. Acid causes serious and lifelong disfigurement which seriously undermines the person's confidence and they often become marginalised due to social ostracism. Acid violence is a criminal offence, but in most cases the perpetrators go unpunished due to inefficiency and reluctance of the police and public prosecutor. The majority of throwers are men and the majority of victim-survivors are women. The Acid Survivors Foundation's research shows that women are attacked for a number of reasons, including: refusing marriage proposals; refusing to develop a relationship; rejecting sexual advances; dowry-related issues; and intra-family disputes over land. The Acid Survivors Foundation provides medical treatment, counselling services, co-ordination of legal services, and support to acid survivors in relation to social reintegration. A second aspect of the organisation's work involves identifying ways to stop acid violence. This involves a wide variety of public education programs and social actions.

The staff at the centre includes nurses, doctors, lawyers, peer counsellors, case managers, counsellors and administrative workers. It is a team that demonstrates considerable dedication. Recently, a staff meeting was held in which Shona Russell and Margaret Ryan facilitated a discussion in relation to the psychological impact on staff on responding to issues of acid violence. Monira Rahman, the Executive Director of the Acid Survivors Foundation, requested this meeting and asked that it attend to four key issues:

- to examine how working in response to acid attacks affects staff;

- to explore ways of dealing with the psychological consequences of working with survivors of acid violence;

- to provide staff with an opportunity to speak about what is important for them in their work; and

- to explore ways in which staff are already responding to the impact of the work and to consider some new possibilities.

Narrative ideas informed how this meeting was structured. We will outline this structure here in the hope that this process may be applicable to other teams of people working in the trauma field.

About the meeting

Twenty staff gathered together in the Acid Survivors Foundation's hospital building and sat in the customary Bangladeshi way, in a circle on the floor. Monira opened the meeting by introducing Margaret and Shona. She spoke about the importance of acknowledging the experiences and difficulties faced by staff, and emphasised the team's interest in exploring what they could do to care for themselves and each other. As there were both Bengali and English speakers present, the meeting was simultaneously translated.

An opening round then took place in which staff members were invited to introduce themselves and to speak about what was important to them in their work. In speaking about what was important to them, the workers told many beautiful stories. These stories drew attention to the particular values that they hold and the hopes they have in relation to responding to the injustice of acid violence. Workers also spoke about the history of their connection to these hopes and told stories of what it means to them to work at the Acid Survivors Foundation. Notes were taken during this discussion and, after the meeting, a document was created from these notes. We've included this document below.

Many people were touched by the stories they heard from their colleagues. Shona described how interested she would have been to interview each person about the values they bring to their work and the histories of these values. She also spoke about her interest in speaking with staff about who in their life would not be surprised to hear them speaking about their work in these ways. The staff members were then asked to consider the following key questions:

- What stood out for you in the stories told by your fellow workers?

- What do these expressions suggest to you about what is important to all of you who work here at the Acid Survivors Foundation?

- Why do you think it is that these particular aspects of people's stories touch you?

- What might you take away from this? How have you been moved by what you heard?

Margaret and Shona then interviewed each other, in front of the staff members, using the categories of outsider-witness response described by Michael White (1999):

1. They described what particular expressions or aspects of the stories had caught their attention.

2. They described what they had found themselves thinking about in regard to the lives of the staff group, and what this suggested to them about what is important to the workers at the Acid Survivors Foundation.

3. They then spoke about what in their own lives or work accounts for why these particular expressions stood out for them.

4. And finally they conveyed how they had been moved on account of witnessing the stories that the staff had shared.

Following this outsider-witness reflection, a short talk was given by Shona about narrative practice. This focused on two themes of particular relevance for workers attending to the consequences of trauma: the significance of eliciting double-storied accounts when responding to those who have been subjected to trauma (see White 2004); and ways in which staff could re-member those people who had fostered the values which are significant to them in their work[2].

In bringing the meeting to a close, a discussion took place about the rich possibilities that arise when workers have the chance to acknowledge each other's values and what is precious to them in the work. The significant skills and knowledge that is demonstrated by survivors of acid violence was also spoken about, as were the contributions that survivors make to workers and to the workplace.

In Bangladesh, at the conclusion of an important meeting, there is often singing and dancing. This meeting concluded with a song, with dancing, with laughter, and the joining of hands.

We hope the structure outlined here, and the document included below, may be of relevance for other teams working in areas in which they are responding to stories of trauma.

A document of the skills, knowledge, experience & values of workers at the Acid Survivors Foundation

This document has been created from conversations shared at the Acid Survivors Foundation, in Dhaka, Bangladesh, on the 27th September 2005. As staff, we came together to speak about what is important to us in working with those who have suffered acid attacks. The following people were present: Dr Rebeka, Mehruba Mukti, Ruksana Begum, Rikta Roy, Gulshan-Ara-Beauty, Monwara Sultana, Ferdousi Huq Lovely, Minu Baroi, Mukti Bala, Tahmina Islam, Shamsul Islam, Fatema Parveen Putul, Arjumand Banu Mili, Runa Laila, Shufala Biswas, Mahmudur Rahman, Salma Parveen, Kakali Adhikari, Margaret Ryan and Shona Russell.

Our work – responding to those who have suffered from violence

In working at the Acid Survivors Foundation, we have come to learn about the effects of acid violence on people's lives. We have learnt about the distress and sorrow that acid violence causes, and we have learned about our own wishes to respond in some way to those who go through these experiences. We seek to bring help to those who have experienced violence and to stand beside them. We seek to provide some relief to those who are in distress. We aim to assist people to make changes to their lives, even if these changes seem small at first. Some of our work involves assisting survivors to find ways to respond to mental stress. Other aspects of our work help to reduce physical disfigurement. For those of us who have survived acid attacks ourselves, it means a lot to us to be able to express our love and feelings for others who have also survived such attacks. We feel as if we are in this together. Importantly, our work involves the promotion of human rights. This is significant to us. It is something we care deeply about.

The special skills of those of us who have survived acid violence ourselves

Those of us who have experienced acid violence and have joined the staff of ASF, bring with us special understandings. We understand the effects that an acid attack can have. We understand that, after an attack, people come here feeling very confused. We understand that survivors will sometimes struggle with severe mental health problems. We also understand the treatments and what they involve because we have been through them. Some of us have had up to seven operations since being attacked. We can explain to survivors how the treatment can help them. We also bring with us other special skills. These skills include knowing how to share our experiences with other survivors in ways that are helpful. We have skills in knowing how to support people in finding their next steps, and in how to help survivors have less mental stress. Importantly, we know from our own experiences what a difference it can make to receive loving care after the attack. For some of us, the loving care we received from our families, or from one or two people, made a big difference to us after we were attacked. This support we received inspires us to work with others. While we cannot give back a previous life, we know that expressions of love and care can make a big difference.

Long histories of commitment to justice

Our commitments to justice have long histories. For some of us, we have cared about these issues from childhood. Many of us have worked for many years in different organisations to support and stand alongside women who have been subjected to acts of violence and abuse. Our efforts are linked to those who have come before us. Women's organisations such as Naripoko have contributed to an awareness of women's experiences of violence and have linked people together in their determination to do something about this. Much of our work is inspired by women who have come before us. They tirelessly raised awareness of the issue of violence against women in Bangladesh and the societal context within which such acts of violence occur, and initiated services in response to this violence. Our work would not be possible without those who came before us.

Standing beside people

We know how important it is for us to be able to stand beside survivors. If someone is standing beside you, then you are not alone. Standing side-by-side with survivors enables us to express love and care for the people with whom we work. We have developed skills in standing beside survivors. This is something we can do and something that makes a difference.

Learning from survivors and sharing their skills and knowledges

People who have been subjected to acid violence have a great deal of knowledge about what is helpful to them. We have learnt that hearing from survivors about their experiences and ideas is important in our work. Once survivors experience being listened to and respected they are also more able to trust us and explore different treatment possibilities.

The healing significance of touch

Acid attacks affect people's mouths, hands and other parts of their bodies that they rely on to live their daily lives. This means that people often have to learn to use their bodies in new ways and to cope with extreme discomfort and pain. In these situations we have learned about the healing significance of touch. Gentle physical touch can give a lot. It helps in creating relationships of trust and comfort.

Acknowledging the challenges and complexities of doing this work

There are many challenges that we face in this work. There is sadness and sometimes we notice our own tears. This is because we care about the people with whom we work. Other times we may become angry about the effects of acid violence, because we have a strong sense of justice. Sometimes we are not sure what to do when people are distressed and confused. We wish to support them because we care about their lives. Sometimes we struggle to find ways to see past the physical disfigurement and to see the person. What is more, when we hear so many stories about violence it can sometimes be overwhelming. When we cannot solve all the problems we hear about, we can temporarily lose touch with a sense of hope. These are some of the different challenges we face. It assists us when these can be named and spoken about. It assists us when we can talk about these together. These are challenges that we all face. When we can face them together it makes a difference.

Taking time and spending time

Many acid survivors remain in our hospital for a very long time. During this time, when survivors are experiencing such confusion and pain, we are alongside them. We spend a long time in their rooms and over weeks and months we sometimes become very close to them. Knowing people over an extended period of time makes a difference. When a survivor first comes in, sometimes it can be hard to see past the disfigurement and the pain. It can be hard to feel anything other than sorrow. Over time though, it becomes possible to know the person differently. We no longer see the disfigurement and instead see the person. We also start to have many more feelings, not just the bad feelings, not just sorrow. We come to know many things that we appreciate about the person and about knowing them.

We are sustained by those with whom we work

It has meant a lot to us meet and get to know women, men and children who have experienced acid violence. Our connections and relationships with survivors have brought a great deal to our own lives. Some of us receive mental strength from our relationships with survivors. We gather strength from them and this assists us to live our lives. For some of us, working with survivors of acid violence can bring a sense of satisfaction to the bottom of our hearts. There is also, at times, a certain 'spirit' that survivors bring to our lives and this is meaningful to us. It can inspire us to do certain things in our own lives, things we might otherwise not have done. The ways in which many survivors can find ways to share, laugh and stay connected with hope, even after the experience of the attack, also means a lot to us. We become curious as to what enables people to cope in these ways. Asking survivors about their skills of survival can contribute to our work. It can assist us in working with those survivors who have lost touch with hope. The connections and relationships that are formed in a human rights organisation like the Acid Survivors Foundation are different to those that can be formed in strictly medical settings. As workers, we are not only providing medical care, we are also working with people for their rights. Being able to combine medical skills in the context of a human rights organisation means we can build different relationships with people. Our workplace can become 'our place' and this brings motivation and great satisfaction. Seeing changes take place in the lives of those with whom we work is also sustaining. When we witness a survivor see the physical changes after an operation, this is significant to us. It can bring a sense of joy. We are sustained by those with whom we work in many different ways.

What it means to work at the Acid Survivors Foundation

It means a lot to us to be working at the Acid Survivors Foundation. It is significant to us to be able to work in an organisation where it is possible to respond in some way to human rights violations. It is also significant to us because a particular working environment has been created here that we value very much.

Closing

This meeting concluded with a song, with dancing, with laughter, and the joining of hands.

Notes

1. For more information about the Acid Survivors Foundation see: www.acidsurvivors.org
2. For more information about re-membering conversations see Russell & Carey (2004).

References

Russell, S. & Carey, M. (Eds) 2004: *Narrative Therapy: Responding to your questions.* Adelaide: Dulwich Centre Publications.

White, M. 1999: 'Reflecting-team work as definitional ceremony revisited.' *Gecko: a journal of deconstruction and narrative ideas in therapeutic practice,* 2:55-82. Republished 2000 in White, M.: *Reflections on Narrative Practice: Essays & interviews* (chapter 4), pp.59-85. Adelaide: Dulwich Centre Publications.

CHAPTER TEN

The story of Ruthi and Miki:

working with a couple when both partners have experienced trauma

by Saviona Cramer and Yael Gershoni

This chapter describes work by two therapists with a heterosexual couple in which both partners had experienced trauma. The man, Miki, had been traumatised ten years earlier in a suicide bombing on the bus on which he was the driver. The woman, Ruthi, had been traumatised in the years since the bombing by Miki's abusive aggression. The therapeutic conversations described here involved ways of addressing the experiences of both partners, while prioritising Ruthi's safety.

Over the years we have met with many people whose primary concern has been trying to respond to traumatic experiences they have been through. This has been true for individuals, but also for couples and families. When one person experiences a powerful trauma there are usually effects in many other people's lives. So much so, that the effects of trauma can come to rule the lives of the entire family.

In this paper we will share a story of our work with a heterosexual couple with whom we have consulted over the last year. Miki and Ruthi were referred to us in relation to a major crisis in their marriage, but the background to this crisis was the considerable trauma that the male partner had been suffering due to a terror attack many years previously. Miki had been the driver of a school bus that was targeted by a suicide bomber. While he only received very minor physical injuries, a number of children on the bus were killed and many were injured. He saw terrible scenes and was extremely traumatised.

Miki was the only adult on the bus. Despite the fact that there was virtually nothing he could have done to prevent the explosion, he felt powerfully responsible and guilty about what had occurred. So much so that he virtually stopped his life. For some years he sat at home doing nothing at all. He stopped working, he couldn't be a partner to his wife, and he found it very difficult to relate to their four children, two of whom are still very young. Miki retreated from the care of his children. It was as if he moved to the side of the family and to the side of life itself.

A serious further effect of the trauma had led to the crisis in their marriage. Miki's experiences post-trauma included being burdened with a heavy load of flash-backs, fears, anxiety and haunting memories. These were draining his ability to deal with even the smallest of matters. Everyday events were becoming a major struggle and within this context Miki had become very aggressive towards Ruthi. It was as if he could no longer deal with any frustrations, disagreements or disappointments. At what he perceived as even the slightest aggravation, Miki became extremely aggressive. While he didn't physically hit Ruthi, he screamed at her, threw furniture around the house and was insulting and accusatory. The smallest difficulty could bring on one of his rampages and the tension in the household had become worse and worse.

This had many effects on Ruthi's life. She felt as if she was losing herself. She had lost confidence in her own beliefs and abilities. She felt that her voice was no longer being heard in the family, and she had taken to walking around the house as if she was treading on eggshells. Ruthi had come to feel completely restrained and as if the entire household was centred around Miki's potential outbursts.

A year before we became involved, Ruthi began seeing a therapist. The therapeutic conversations they shared were valuable to Ruthi and they have continued to this day. After a year of these consultations, a social worker from the Social Security department who had been assigned to the family since the bus bombing, spoke to Miki and told him that he had to take action if he wanted his relationship with Ruthi and his children to continue. While Miki was very suspicious of the idea of therapy, they both came to meet with us. Ruthi continued to see her own therapist, where we knew she had a chance to speak about her own experiences of the abuse. We were asked specifically to try to address the relationship issues.

We knew it was going to be important to take care in relation to Ruthi's experience of the couple therapy. Throughout the process described below we would have periodic discussions with Ruthi's individual therapist. At times, we would also hold sessions in which the two of us, Ruthi, Miki and Ruthi's therapist would all meet together. These processes then enabled us to work with the stories of Ruthi's experience and also Miki's earlier experience of trauma.

Working as a duo

Recently, we have been working together with certain couples. Having both of us in the room enables all sorts of options for interviewing, reflecting and discussing ideas in front of the couple, and we have found this flexibility very rewarding. In situations where a man has been violent and/or abusive, it can also be reassuring to have each other in the room.

In working with Miki and Ruthi, our teamwork made many sorts of explorations possible. First of all, we were both able to ask questions and we often came up with different lines of enquiry. Secondly, after we had listened to their responses, we could turn to each other and reflect upon what we had heard. Thirdly, we could then ask Miki and Ruthi to reflect upon what we had said. And then we could continue with asking them further questions. It was as if all four of us were investigating the effects of trauma in their lives. And a team of four investigators can get a lot done!

A philosophy of externalisation

While Ruthi had already participated in counselling, for Miki this was a very new experience and one that was foreign to him. It was clear to us that he was frightened of losing Ruthi and very unsure about what it meant to attend therapy. It seemed important to us to ensure from the very first interaction with both Miki and Ruthi that they experienced us as respectful of their knowledge, skills and ideas, and that all the difficulties they were going through were spoken about in externalising language (Freedman & Combs 2002). If we were to assist Miki in finding ways to deal with both the trauma he had been subject to, and the aggression he had demonstrated to Ruthi, we needed to ensure that he felt comfortable in talking with us, and that he knew we respected his intellect and hopes for his life.

Creating a context for Ruthi to speak

The first step, it seemed to us, was to assist Miki to learn how to listen, to create a context in which Ruthi could speak about her experiences of recent times. This required some work because, at first, Ruthi had difficulty in speaking. In fact, one of the first things that Ruthi described was that these days she found herself feeling paralysed and unable to speak. She was very concerned as to how Miki would respond to what she had to say, that he would feel insulted and offended, that it could make things worse rather than better.

There were a number of ways that we approached this situation. As it happened, when we asked Miki and Ruthi what had been going on for them, Miki suggested that Ruthi speak first. We asked Miki about this curiosity and openness that he had to listen to Ruthi's experience. We asked him questions about why this was meaningful to him.

We also became very curious about what would enable Miki to listen. We would speak with each other, in front of them both, speculating about what it would mean if we could all have the chance to hear more about Ruthi's life. We speculated about what effects it might have on each of us if Ruthi was able to describe in detail what she had been going through. During this time we always spoke in externalising language and never gave the impression that we would be blaming Miki for the problems that had been so pervasive recently. We simply became curious about Miki's curiosity, until it got to the point where he was well prepared to listen and try to understand the intricacies of Ruthi's experiences.

An outsider-witness context

Once we felt that Miki was ready, we set up a particular structure in which he could listen and respond to Ruthi's experiences. We decided that we would interview Ruthi with Miki being a witness to the conversation. We took care to invite Miki into a particular witnessing position (White 2004a). We asked Miki to step into a position of a friend to Ruthi so that, while he was listening to her describe her experiences, he would listen with a friend's ear. Rather than trying to listen as the person whose actions had caused Ruthi harm and sadness, rather than listening as her husband, we asked him if he could simply listen as a friend would listen. We asked him to imagine that Ruthi was a friend of his who had come to tell him these stories. We asked him if he thought he would be able to listen without arguing or becoming defensive.

Miki thought that this would be possible. We arranged for ways of interrupting the process if things were not going well, and we described that down the track in future consultations Miki would have a chance to be interviewed with Ruthi as a witness.

This process made it possible for Miki to hear for the first time what life had become like for Ruthi. It also made it possible for Miki to respond in non-defensive ways, and this made a real difference to the process.

The effects of trauma

When Ruthi started to talk, she began to describe how frightened she had become when Miki was around. She spoke about how she now tries to make herself as small as she can, how she tries not to talk too much. The effects of the abuse were so severe to Ruthi that she had even started to stutter. She had started to become muddled in her language and was mixing her words due to fear. Ruthi described this in detail. She told us that, when she was about to say something, she regularly stopped herself by thinking: 'Don't, he will scream at you, so don't'. Ruthi also described how she would routinely take the children away, out of the house, whenever they looked as if they were going to misbehave, or to cry or yell, in order to avoid them facing an outburst from Miki.

When Miki offered reflections on what he had heard, he spoke as a friend and acknowledged how very difficult life had been for Ruthi. He also described that he was shocked. He said that he had had no idea what a big effect the aggression was having on Ruthi. He knew he had been angry, and that he had screamed a little bit, but then after each of these instances he would calm down and think 'what is the big deal?' Now though, he said, this was the first time he had started to see the effect of the trauma, to really understand what had been going on. He described that he had no idea how bad Ruthi's life and the children's lives had been – that they cannot play, cannot cry, cannot run. He said it sounded as if they were paralysed within the house.

It seemed clear to us that Miki was listening to Ruthi in a way that he had not done previously and that this listening was opening space for him to understand his own actions differently. We discovered later that the trauma Miki had been through had in some way made him centred in his own difficulties. He had become unaware of the effects of his actions on others. In order for Miki to be able to begin to take responsibility for his actions, we needed to find a way in which he could step out of centring his own experience. We all decided that it would be important for Miki to hear more about Ruthi's experiences and this took up a number of sessions.

Taking a position

It was meaningful for Miki to realise that the trauma he had experienced was living on, not only in his life, but also in the lives of his partner and children. After listening to Ruthi, he made a decision that he did not want to give the trauma such a large place in his life. He wanted to claim his own life back, not only for his sake, but for the sake of Ruthi and the future of his children. He described this quite clearly by saying: 'I went through some very difficult things in my life (the bombing). I realise now that if I deal with this I will be able to manage the anger that is now causing such harm. I will do this. I promise you.'

When Ruthi first heard these words, however, they did not mean much to her. She had no faith that Miki was capable of making these changes. These just sounded like words to her. It was up to us to continue to create a context whereby Miki could address the effects of the trauma on his life, and take steps to address the anger and aggression that had been tyrannising Ruthi's life and the lives of the children. It was up to us to create a context to enable Miki to control the anger, instead of the anger controlling his life and the life of his family.

An opening for Miki to speak about his experiences of trauma

In tracing the history of how aggression had come to play such a large part in Miki's life, we began to hear how it was connected to the bus bombing that had occurred ten years previously. Miki had never really spoken about his experience of this before. A particular opening occurred when Ruthi started to speak about how she needed Miki to begin taking more responsibility and care of the children. It was only then that Miki started to explain his experiences in relation to the children, how he found it impossible to listen to the children crying, how it transported him back to the scene of the bombing even now, ten years later. This was a revelation to Ruthi. She had had absolutely no idea that the sounds of children crying and screaming evoked for Miki the images of the bombing and were so distressing to him.

With Ruthi as a witness, Miki started to tell his story about the way he lives, about his experience of life. In the course of these interviews, it became clear that Miki himself hadn't realised that the bus bombing had affected him in so many ways. He hadn't realised that things were getting worse and worse. We created space for Miki to be able to honestly speak about the range of effects that the bombing of the bus had had on his life. So much of his life now seemed out of control and out of his hands. Being able to trace these developments and link them back to the bombing of the bus, put them in a particular timeline and in some way diminished their all-pervasive powers. It was as if a possible explanation was emerging for all that had gone awry in his life.

Alternative stories

We then became interested to explore openings to alternative stories, stories that would provide some sort of antidote to the story of trauma and the effects of aggression. Three themes began to emerge: 'talking together', 'living a more equal life', and 'sharing the care of the children'. These themes represented what Ruthi and Miki wanted for their life.

Talking together

We discovered that when Miki and Ruthi were a young couple they would talk together about everything. But this ended after the bus bombing. After this traumatic event, there were things that Miki did not know how to convey and the communication between them, the sharing of their lives, ceased. It seemed that Miki had been tricked into the idea that in order for him to be strong he needed to deal with the effects of the trauma on his own. This debilitating idea, which appears to descend on so many people after traumas (particularly men), had stopped him talking to Ruthi [see box]. As the therapy consultations initiated new ways of talking together, we began to witness a regeneration of dialogue and conversation between Miki and Ruthi. In each session we would inquire about the sorts of discussions they had been having at home since the last time we had seen them. We would ask them how they had gone about having these conversations. We came to see that re-learning how to talk and listen to each other was a key part of reclaiming their relationship from the effects of trauma and aggression. 'Talking together' became an alternative

The effect of trauma on communication

This theme relating to how trauma affects communication and conversations between people has arisen many times in our consultations. We have heard from many people that they have decided not to share some of their experiences related to trauma due to wanting to protect their partner. They have not wanted their partner to suffer from what they experienced and so they have sheltered them by only telling them certain details. We have also heard people describe that after a traumatic event they have felt that it would be impossible to explain the experience, that it was pointless even trying because there is no way that another person could possibly understand what it had been like. They regularly describe that the experience was 'beyond words', that 'words cannot convey' what they went through. We have also witnessed how difficult it can be for some people to speak. We have seen how this manifests itself physically, through sweating, trembling. We never infer or assume that someone has to describe the full details of the trauma in order to heal from this experience. We are careful not to cause re-traumatisation. If the person wishes to speak about the details of the event then we certainly respond to this, but it is not an imperative on our part. However, finding ways to address the effects of the trauma on people's communication, on their links with others, on the ways they speak about their lives, does seem highly significant. This is a different task and can be a key aspect of reducing the sense of isolation and hopelessness that can accompany experiences of trauma.

theme that grew richer and richer as the therapy continued. Its history was traced and the skills it involved were described, remembered and brought back to their daily lives.

Living a more equal life

In talking with both Ruthi and Miki, we asked a number of questions about the future of their relationship, how they envisaged their marriage, their relationship, what they wanted for their lives, what they wanted for their children's lives. Miki described how he really wanted a partnership in which he could talk to his wife, and listen to her, seek her advice. He wanted a relationship in which they could share their worries and ideas. In speaking about this, he realised that if he was not able to control his anger then their relationship would never be like the partnership that he wanted to have. A theme that began to emerge from these enquiries was one of 'living a more equal life'. Both Miki and Ruthi spoke about their desire for their relationship to become more equal, for Ruthi's voice and skills to be elevated in the household. Interestingly, a key step in the development of this story about 'living a more equal life' involved Miki's business.

For some years after the bomb attack, Miki had not worked at all. But recently he had turned a long-standing hobby into a small business. For many years he had been interested in car-detailing, in redecorating cars in different styles. He had realised that he could sell redecorated cars for much more than he purchased them. He had also begun to build cars from scratch. For Miki, one aspect of 'living a more equal life' involved encouraging Ruthi to begin to work with him in his business. Ruthi was hesitant at first. She did not believe she had anything to offer the business. She would say that she only knew how to clean, that this was the only work that she could do. And yet Miki was encouraging. He would say: 'But you are so clever. I want you to use your intelligence. I know that you could become a partner in this business. You could run the office. You could learn how to use a computer.' And with this encouragement and assistance she learnt. While she knew nothing about business to start with, they now run the business together and it is Ruthi who decides how to spend the money, who to pay first, how the finances are distributed.

Sharing the care of the children

As Ruthi began to work outside the home, she was very clear that she needed Miki to become more active and responsible in relation to the care of their children. This was complicated for two reasons. Firstly, as we've already mentioned, the effects of the trauma that Miki had experienced in the past had made him frightened and overwhelmed by the children's screaming and crying. And secondly, he literally did not know how to care for them. Just as Miki made a pledge to address his anger and its effects, he also made a decision to try to become closer to his children, to change the way he was relating to them.

This took some time. First of all, we needed to respond to the effects of the trauma. Having listened to Ruthi describe her experiences, Miki felt more able to talk about all he had been going through. He described to us the images that would come to him whenever he heard the crying of children. These were images of wounded and dying children. He also described how terribly ashamed he was that he couldn't deal with this. He felt such a failure that he was still having these vivid responses. Ruthi had had no idea about this, and not knowing had led to tension and anger between them. For Miki to be able to explain to Ruthi his experience of this, to speak about how he felt afraid and vulnerable at these times, and that he simply didn't know what to do about it, was transformative. What he couldn't do alone, they could do together. Ruthi was so relieved to understand what had been going on and became very supportive in relation to this. Once they were not polarised, and once the problem was externalised, they had a chance to work together on this, step by step. Gradually Miki started to take more steps to care for their children.

A second issue then became apparent. Miki had become so disconnected from children and children's ways of being that he literally did not know how to care for the children. Some of the therapy sessions became focused on this. Miki honestly said to Ruthi that he had no idea what to do with the children. When Ruthi said: 'When you come home you're supposed to give them a bath, give them dinner, and then put them to bed', Miki replied: 'But what do you mean give them a bath, dinner and put them to bed? Do you know how complicated these things are for me? How do you put them to bed? At what time? Perhaps these are simple things to you but they are not for me! Please tell me the small things I need to do, even if you think they are so obvious because you are so used to doing them. Please help me to see how I can be more part of raising the children.'

Some quite detailed conversations then took place in which Miki would ask about how Ruthi knows when the children are hungry or tired or irritated, or even happy. He would ask questions about what would seem to be very simple things, such as: 'Well, what is dinner for these children?' Some of these conversations were very funny. They were also honouring of Ruthi's skills and knowledge. Importantly, because Miki had assisted Ruthi to learn about working in the business, there was a history that could be built upon: 'This is okay', Miki said once, 'When you came into the office you didn't know about certain things that were very easy for me. I had to explain to you how to do the bookwork, how to use the computer, and now you can do all of this. That's what this is like, but in reverse, and in the home.'

While it took some time, Miki now takes up a much greater responsibility in relation to the children's lives. He now experiences fewer flashbacks or recurring imagery when the children cry or scream. Even when the flashbacks return, he now has ways of dealing with these, of minimising their impact, and can continue to respond to the child concerned.

Acknowledging values

We also created space for both Ruthi and Miki to articulate the values that were important to them and which they wanted to inform their lives and relationship. We asked Miki what he values in his relationships as a partner, as a father, as a friend, why he wants to take particular steps, why they are important for him. In trying to respond to these questions, Miki would tell us that he had never thought about these sorts of things before.

The questions were at times challenging for Ruthi also. She described at first that she felt under so much pressure that she didn't think it was time to dream. She said she hadn't had the time to even think about what she wants for herself, what she values or what her dreams might be. She was used to just trying to get through day-after-day. But, in time, she could describe what was significant to her, why she so wanted to survive these experiences, what she was living for, and the histories that inform these wishes.

In response to our questions, Ruthi spoke of how her first priority in life was her family. This was a value that was connected to her background. She had been very close to her parents and, when they had died, her sisters had become her closest friends. Whenever they needed anything they would be there for each other. Ruthi described how she wanted her immediate family, with Miki and their children, to be a similar united family. This was not an experience she had ever had with Miki. Up until the time of therapy, Ruthi used to spend any free time with her family, while Miki's social life was completely engaged with male friends who Ruthi did not know. Sometimes she would even find strange men in the family home who Miki had invited over without introducing to her. Gradually, through the course of counselling, this changed. The relationships of their immediate family came to receive a greater priority and began to flourish as a result.

Taking time

As we mentioned earlier, Ruthi was seeing her own counsellor throughout this process, and this counsellor, quite rightly, was completely focused on her experience. Their sessions together were a separate place where the effects of the abuse could be discussed and where Ruthi could think through the decisions she was making and whether or not she wished to remain in the relationship. Initially, Ruthi was not at all confident about Miki making real changes and getting his anger and aggression under control. As Miki came to understand more about her experiences, he tried to convince Ruthi that he had changed. In our sessions together he would sometimes check in with her, asking her whether she had noticed the changes that he was making. And she would reply: 'Yes, I do … but it's only been a short time so far … I cannot know yet whether these changes are going to be permanent'. Understandably, she has needed to see longer term changes. It has only been relatively recently that she has come to the conclusion that he has made real changes, and that he is in some ways 'a different man' from the one he had become after the bombing. But the road to get to this point has not always been easy. It seems relevant to mention some of the ups and downs that occurred along the way.

A setback?

There was a particular session in which Miki became very angry during the therapy conversations. Ruthi was trying to describe her experience when Miki became very defensive and then very angry. When we tried to ask questions about this anger and his expression of it, Miki spoke in a fury: 'I'm not screaming! I am just making a point! She's wrong, I'm right, and I'm making a point until she will realise that she's wrong!' It was a stark moment. Ruthi was devastated. Miki had thought that he was making meaningful progress and, when he suddenly saw himself through our eyes, he realised how much more needed to occur. We tried to make the most of this occurrence. We asked questions about how this fury had come into the room. We asked Miki about the effects of this fury and the effects of his justifications. We asked Miki about how he could become so out of touch with what he was feeling and saying. And we asked about what was going to need to happen in order for Ruthi to feel confident in expressing her own thoughts. Having witnessed Miki's fury, we had a greater appreciation of Ruthi's experience. In talking about this, Miki also realised that he didn't like who he became in those moments. While it seemed a setback at the time, it also proved to be a turning-point. From this moment onwards, Miki had a much greater recognition of the effects of his actions.

Acknowledging Ruthi's trauma

While Ruthi was still trying to decide whether she would stay in the relationship, at times Miki would become impatient. He would say to her things like: 'I need your warmth'. Ruthi had lived with the trauma of Miki's anger for ten years. Now that he had realised more about the effects of his actions he had become very warm and caring towards Ruthi, but it was taking her time to work out what she wanted, and what these changes meant. Ten years is a very long time to be traumatised by the man with whom you are living, and with whom you have children.

What seemed most important in relation to this was to find ways for Ruthi to able to convey the extent of her trauma. As Miki became more sensitised to how the trauma he had experienced had affected all aspects of his life, he also became more sensitive to Ruthi's experiences. We interviewed Ruthi, with Miki as a witness, about certain memories that would return to her and haunt her. These were memories of particular incidences that she could not forget, that she could not confine to the past. For instance, there was one time when Miki had been worried that Ruthi was going to leave him and he had locked her in the house and then left. Ruthi was left locked in the house for a few days. She was too embarrassed to call people to tell them what had occurred and she felt humiliated.

A turning-point occurred when the two of them went on a vacation together. The money for this family vacation was provided by Social Security. They stayed in a hotel that they had visited two years previously. On this earlier trip Miki had treated Ruthi very badly. When they re-entered the foyer of the hotel, Ruthi said to him: 'Do you remember this spot? Do you remember what happened between us here? When I am here I can still feel the tension and sorrow in my stomach.' And yet they had a good time together on this trip and, when it came to the end of their time away, Ruthi felt differently. She said: 'Now that I also have good memories of this place, my feelings have changed'. She told us that this was the first time that she began to feel some hope for the future.

There was still an important process to occur. As Ruthi had felt so unsafe for many years, she needed to convey to Miki that she could no longer tolerate even small outbursts of anger from him. She needed to convey that, whenever he was angry now, it resonated with all the bad times and she could not cope with this. Fortunately, Miki could understand this. He said that he thought this was similar to the reasons why he couldn't tolerate his children crying. The cries of children reminded him of the trauma he experienced, and so he continued to work on controlling his anger so that he could be someone that Ruthi could appreciate living with. He realised that this was going to be a long process. He came to realise that Ruthi needed a great deal of time for this. He learnt patience. It was a patience that grew from an understanding of the trauma to which Ruthi had been subjected.

Reflections

Our conversations with Ruthi and Miki are continuing. Their story is an example for us of the ways in which one traumatic event can influence the stories of many people's lives. It is also an example of needing to work with different people on varying stories of trauma. Ruthi had experienced the trauma of Miki's aggression over ten years. Miki had experienced the trauma of the bomb blast ten years ago.

The use of externalising conversations, outsider-witness practices and re-authoring conversations, all enabled the effects of trauma to be named and explored. They also enabled the generation of a number of alternative stories of 'talking together', 'living a more equal life' and 'sharing the care of the children'.

Over the last ten years, our work at the Barcai Institute in Tel Aviv has increasingly involved responding to the effects of trauma and bereavement. At present, about half of our work relates to these matters. The trauma of a suicide bombing always effects far more people than those who are killed or wounded. As therapists, we see continuing effects on families and communities. As the story of Ruthi and Miki demonstrates, sometimes these effects ripple on for many years. In responding to these families, we are trying to develop ways of working that prioritise issues of safety. We are very careful not to cause re-traumatisation by pushing a person to talk about what happened to him or her, while at the same time enabling re-authoring work to take place with all concerned. We hope this paper offers a glimpse of these continuing efforts.

References and related reading

Freedman, J. & Combs, G. (eds) 2002: *Narrative Therapy with Couples ... and a whole lot more! A collection of papers, essays and exercises.* Adelaide: Dulwich Centre Publications.

White, M. 2004a: 'Narrative practice, couple therapy and conflict dissolution.' In White, M.: *Narrative Practice & Exotic Lives: Resurrecting diversity in everyday life* (chapter 1), pp. 1-41. Adelaide: Dulwich Centre Publications.

White, M. 2004b: 'Working with people who are suffering the consequences of multiple trauma: A narrative perspective.' *International Journal of Narrative Therapy and Community Work,* 1:45-76.

CHAPTER ELEVEN

Stories from Robben Island:

a report from a journey of healing

by David Denborough

What principles and practices can contribute to a 'Healing of memories' in countries and communities that have experienced widespread trauma and violence? A three-day gathering on Robben Island, South Africa, brought participants together from many different parts of the world to share stories and ideas about the healing of memories and ways to address histories of trauma. This chapter describes some of the principles and practices of healing which shaped this meeting. It describes the structure of story-telling and reflection that occurred, and includes a number of stories, reflections and the lyrics of songs to convey the experience.

Picture if you can, a ferry making its way at night from Cape Town to Robben
Island off the shore of South Africa. On board are about 70 people from many
different countries including Uganda, Rwanda, Namibia, Samoa, Zambia,
Zimbabwe, Lesotho, Germany, Burundi, Eritrea, Northern Ireland, the USA,
Australia and from South Africa. Their experiences of life are vastly different
from each other, but all have at least one thing in common: a determination
to find ways to contribute towards the healing of histories of trauma that have
occurred in their respective countries.

This group of people came together for three days on Robben Island,
and appropriately the gathering began on South Africa's election day. The
histories of South Africa set an inspiring context for the conversations that
were to take place:

> *Given over three centuries of repeated violations of human rights*
> *– from the decimation of the first people by early settlers, through*
> *slavery, bloodshed, forced removals and the incarceration of the*
> *leadership of our liberation movements – Cape Town and its*
> *people have experienced much pain and suffering. But we have*
> *also seen hope and the triumph of the human spirit – on our*
> *streets, in our Parliament and, we hope, in our hearts and homes.*

These were words from the Mayor of Cape Town, Nomaindiya
Mfeketo, as she welcomed participants to this event. The South Africans
amongst us had come straight from the polling booths and many poignantly
described what this meant to them: 'It makes me very emotional to have voted
now for the third time. I will not wash this ink from my thumb for quite some
time. It will act as a reminder that I can vote and all that this means.'

Robben Island, where the gathering was held, was the place where the
leadership of the South African liberation movements, including Nelson
Mandela, were imprisoned for many years. The prison on the island stands as
a monument to the histories of resistance that culminated in the
transformation of South Africa. When you stand on the island, looking out
over the water back towards Cape Town and the majestic Table Mountain, so
many images come to mind. During the gathering we were constantly aware

of the contributions of so many South Africans to address the injustice of Apartheid. We were also aware of the many lives that were lost along the way.

Background

This 'Journey to Healing and Wholeness Conference' was the initiative of the Institute for the Healing of Memories and the Desmond Tutu Peace Centre. The work of the Institute for the Healing of Memories grew out of Fr Michael Lapsley's work as Chaplain at the Cape Town Trauma Centre. Part of the Chaplaincy project there involved developing a way of bringing people together to address the trauma of South Africa's past. The Healing of Memories workshops they created were designed as a parallel process to the Truth and Reconciliation Commission.

Over time, Fr Michael Lapsley and the Institute for the Healing of Memories were invited to host similar workshops in other countries. Over the last five years, to assist participants to address traumatic histories, these workshops have taken place in New York City, Rwanda, Eritrea, Sri Lanka, Zimbabwe, Germany, Uganda, Burundi, Northern Ireland, East Timor and Australia.

This gathering on Robben Island was designed as an opportunity for people who had participated in Healing of Memories workshops in their own countries to come together, to share experiences and stories and to learn from one another. The stories told were also to be documented in the written word, on video and in song so that they could be made available to others.

The structure of the gathering

The entire gathering was influenced by the metaphor of a journey. It was clearly stated that we did not know exactly where the conversations would lead, and that we would end up somewhere that we could not anticipate. At the same time, however, there was a very carefully developed structure which would shape the conversations that were to take place. This structure consisted of five parts.

Part One: An interview

Each session began with an interview in which either Father Michael Lapsley or Glenda Wildschut would interview two participants. These two participants would have been chosen well in advance and they would be invited to share their own stories around a particular theme. These interviews would take place in a large circle with all participants as witnesses.

Part Two: Small group reflections

As soon as the interview finished, the participants would then move into small groups of 8-10 people in each of which was a facilitator and a scribe. These small groups provided an opportunity for all participants to speak about what witnessing the interviews in Part One had meant to them, how they could relate to the stories that had been told, and what they learnt from them. There was also the opportunity for people to share something of their own journey around the particular theme that was being discussed. Approximately an hour was spent in these small groups.

Part Three: Large group reflections

Everyone would then reconvene in the large circle and a series of reflections would take place. The first of these was in the form of a song that had been written from the words spoken by those who had been interviewed in Part One. Following the song, three appointed people would offer their reflections on the interviews that everyone had heard, and then there would be an opportunity for any of the participants to share further reflections in the large group.

Part Four: Final words

Space was always then created for the people who had been interviewed in Part One to make final comments on their experiences of the process.

This four stage structure was then repeated as two more people were interviewed around a different theme.

Themes

Four themes were considered during the first two days of the gathering. These were:

i)   Voices of those who have lived on death row.

ii) Exploring experiences of shame and guilt.

iii) Stories of transcendence.

iv) Stories of reconciliation.

Principles and practices of healing

Many of the stories that were told during the three days were accounts of considerable trauma. And yet, I believe that everyone present appreciated the event as significantly healing. While part of the explanation for this relates to the fact that the vast majority of participants had already been through a healing of memories workshop in their own country, I wish here to outline a number of principles and practices of healing that occurred during the gathering that contributed to creating a meaningful and significant event. I am sure there were many other principles and practices that were informing the actions of the facilitators and organisers of this event that I have not included in this short paper. Those that I have listed below are simply the practices and principles that I particularly noticed and valued.

Journey metaphor

At all times, the gathering was constructed around the metaphor of a journey. By constructing a process of 'healing' as a journey, this implied movement, changes of territory, and an attention to differences of experience over time. When people were interviewed in front of the group, the interviewers took care to ask about the differences in experiences of the past in comparison to the present. They also took care to elicit the different stages of a person's journey, including the most difficult periods as well as the passages of relief. The themes of the gathering – 'coming to terms with shame and guilt', 'transcendence' and 'reconciliation' – also conveyed movement. In these ways, we were all invited to consider ourselves to be on a journey, one that would not be completed over these days but that would continue into our futures. This orientation captured participants' imagination and encouraged us to revisit the territories we have passed through in our lives, the ground we are currently standing upon, and the directions we wish to explore in the future.

The four part story-telling structure

The structure outlined above enabled all participants to have the opportunity to listen, reflect and share stories. Importantly, the structure enabled movement from individual story, to small group, to large group discussion, and this generated a sense of connection. What's more, participants joined the same small group each time throughout the three days and this built a sense of cohesion. As there was a facilitator in each small group this enabled the organisers to have a good sense of how everyone was experiencing the process and to respond accordingly.

Healing as action

Throughout the three days there was an emphasis on action as a healing response to trauma. For instance, when people were interviewed in front of the group, the interviewers took care to elicit the steps that people had taken to respond to the trauma they had experienced. Those who were interviewed had all taken a range of steps to respond to the trauma to which they were subjected. This action was not limited to their own lives but included steps that they were taking to either respond to the trauma experienced by others, or to try to prevent others' experience of trauma. This orientation to healing as action opened space for participants to acknowledge their own actions in response to trauma and also to consider possibilities for future actions and collaborations.

More than individual experience

In a range of ways throughout the three days, care was taken to link any individual's experience of pain or hardship to broader collective experience.

While it was a caring environment, it was a caring with a collective spirit. When people were interviewed in front of the group, the interviewers took care to elicit not only the individual person's story but also how this fitted with the broader group or collective to which this person belonged. It also made a difference that two people were interviewed in front of the group in Stage One. The interviewers would turn from one person to another at certain points in the interview. This meant that there was never an over-attendance to any individual's story and instead the emphasis was on building links between stories and experiences. Similarly, the journey of healing was not constructed as a journey simply for individuals to take, but one in which we had responsibilities to our broader communities. It became clear that all of us were present, not simply as individuals, but as representatives of broader groups of people. The documentation process was also a part of this. People were gathering together not only to share their stories with each other but to document these in ways that would hopefully be of assistance to others.

The linking of stories

The four part structure outlined above contributed to a sense of linking the stories told by those interviewed in front of the group to the stories of other participants. The process of the telling of stories and then inviting reflections in response enabled a sense of connectedness between peoples of many different lands, and this acted as an antidote to the isolation that so often accompanies experiences of trauma. Significantly, as people shared stories of their 'journeys' – their ups and downs, and learnings along the way – this offered participants a sense of comradeship as well as opportunities to learn from each other.

Space to speak about having done harm

One of the practices of healing during the gathering that stood out to me was the commitment by the facilitators to create space for people to speak about times in which they may have done harm to others. Even for those who may have been subjected to trauma themselves, space was created for them to consider and speak about actions towards others that they may sincerely regret. Michael Lapsley has described that:

> ... *during the Apartheid years, to be a decent human being in South Africa required heroism, and most of us are not heroes ... and so when apartheid was finally overthrown, it was hardly surprising that so many of us, both black and white, struggled to find ways of understanding how we acted towards others and how others acted towards us during those times.* (2002, p.72).

This orientation, and the determination to enable everyone the opportunity to come to terms with actions they may regret, enabled stories to be told that otherwise would not have been shared.

Acknowledging complexity

As participants were able to speak of the experiences of their lives, this created opportunities for the acknowledgement of various complexities. This was perhaps best illustrated in the session on reconciliation which began with Andrew Rice being interviewed about his brother's death in the World Trade Centre on September 11th and his subsequent work with the group September 11 Families for Peaceful Tomorrows. Pat Magee was then interviewed about his involvement with the IRA and subsequent reconciliation work with the daughter of one of the men who was killed in a bombing that Pat was involved in organising.

Listening alternatively to the stories of Andrew, whose brother was killed in a terrorist attack, and then Pat who was involved in carrying out a terrorist attack and spoke of still believing in the necessity of armed struggle at certain times and places, invited us all into considering the complexities, politics and values associated with many experiences of trauma and the ways in which we respond to them.

The fact that these conversations were taking place in South Africa invited further reflection – we were all conscious that we were within a country in which the African National Congress, under Nelson Mandela, had turned to armed resistance (all be it with considerable care taken to minimise casualties) when other forms of action had not succeeded.

Humour

On numerous occasions, it made a difference that the organisers had a very cheeky sense of humour. It was clearly demonstrated from the start of the gathering that even though we were there to discuss stories and experiences of great sorrow, there would also be considerable laughter.

Silence

Moments of silence were also utilised in simple but significant ways. At different times in the proceedings, especially after someone had told a powerful story, and prior to the participants moving into small groups, the facilitator would simply request a moment's silence. This silence contributed to the ceremonial aspect of the meeting and in some ways offered a sense of reverence to the story just told.

Invitation to consider our own healing traditions

On the final morning of the gathering, a presentation from Loudeen Parsons from Samoa/New Zealand, invited participants from different countries to consider their own culture's rituals, values and symbols of healing and reconciliation:

> *I invite you to explore your own cultures for its rituals, values and richness on the subjects of forgiveness and reconciliation. In our experience, apology, forgiveness and reconciliation is not only or primarily personal or intra-psychic – it is about restoring the wellbeing of relationships between people and people, people and their ancestry, people and their Gods, and people and the environment. Finding ways to excavate the liberative cultural*

elements and rituals of reconciliation from our own cultures seems a vital aspect of this work. In the process, we are asking ourselves the following questions: How do we grow cultures of reconciliation? How do we tell the young of atrocities that took place? How do we not lose sight of atrocities and yet at the same time be free of the pain that goes with it?

This invitation resonated for many participants and contributed to thoughtful explorations.

Involvement of young people

On the final morning of the conference a group of young people, who had been completing a parallel 'Healing of Memories' process in their schools, drummed, sang, danced and clapped their way into the centre of the meeting hall. Their energy and enthusiasm was inspiring to everyone present. They shared with us their perspectives on dealing with the past and moving into the future and this provided a powerful sense of continuity. They ended their presentation as they had begun it, singing: Young people of Africa / Freedom is in your hands / Show us the way to freedom / In this land of Africa.

Use of song

As mentioned earlier, songs were crafted from the words that people spoke during the four-part story-telling structure and these songs were then sung as reflections. In creating the lyrics to these songs, a particular emphasis was given to including words that described the responses that people had made to trauma, the values which shaped these responses, and the histories which have informed these values (see White 2004). When the poetic and evocative phrases that people use to tell the stories of their lives are placed into melodies, they become in some way more memorable, more significant, embodied in a different way. When these songs are recorded they can then be played at any time providing an ongoing reminder of a person's particular journey and the skills and knowledges they have accumulated along the way

(Denborough 2002).The songs that were written during the gathering were recorded while we were on Robben Island. Two of these were recorded collectively so that everyone could hear their own voice on the CD that was given to participants at the end of the three days.

Written documentation

A written document was also given to each participant on the final day. This contained stories and reflections that had been told during the conference. This written document did not include everything that was said. It aimed to be selective and yet representative of the key themes and stories that had been shared. Particular emphasis was given to stories or practices of healing that had been identified. In this way, participants left the gathering with their own words documented in both the written word and in song.

One example of the process

It is not the aim of this piece to convey the stories that were shared during this conference as these will be available soon on the website of the Institute for the Healing of Memories: www.healingofmemories.co.za

However, in order to convey how the process worked, it seems important to provide an example of the interweaving of stories.

On the first morning of conference, Elias Wanyama and Duma Kumalo were interviewed and spoke about how they had survived their experiences on death row. I have included here the stories that they told; some reflections that were spoken in the small groups in response to these stories; the song that was created from the words of Elias and Duma; some reflections that were offered by other participants in the large group; and then some closing words from Duma and Elias. I hope this will convey something of the process.

Part One: Stories from Death Row

Duma Kumalo and Elias Wanyama were interviewed about their experiences on death row.

Reaching hearts
Elias Wanyama

To be a former prisoner and to come here to Robben Island, what is a former prison, is quite an extraordinary thing for me. I am from Uganda and twenty years ago I joined the national security personnel and became involved in the repression of the Ugandan people. I thought this was all right at the time. I felt justified in arresting and imprisoning others until the tables turned and I myself was arrested. This posed to me the first great challenge of my life. Suddenly I was face-to-face with those I had arrested. They were looking at me as their captor. Some years later I was sentenced to death and I lived on death row for nine years. I was in prison for 18years. Death row involves waiting for death, knowing it could come any minute, any day. My entire time on the row of death was a struggle for hope, for when the electricity of hope is turned off, the bulb of life dies.

Now, I have no grudge, but at the time I was sentenced to death, if I could have fought my way out of the situation I would have. There were also times in those years when I would have welcomed death. I was overwhelmed with a sense of hopelessness. For me, what opened the door to hope was a spiritual journey. I still remember one day hearing men singing praises to God while on their way to the gallows. Their demonstration of hope and faith and how it meant they could sing on the way to their death, meant everything to me. It kindled a faith within me and this was the starting-point in turning my life around.

On death row in Uganda there was no system, as far as I could see, as to who was executed and who remained alive. We did not know when someone would be taken to die. This sense of chaos was very difficult to live with. There was really only one thing that was constant and that was the message from our dying friends to those left behind. They would always simply say: 'Tell the world'.

I now work for an organisation called 'Friends of hope for condemned prisoners'. There are still over 550 people on death row in Uganda and we are working to end the death penalty and to support the families of those who are on death row. Often the families of prisoners are victimised and many have to leave society. I owe this work to those who have been executed, to those who are on death row now, and to those who might be on death row in the future.

Despite this work that gives my life meaning, I cannot say that I am happy. When I was released I still had nightmares of being hanged. I would wake up at night screaming through my teeth. It has been very difficult trying to relate back to my family. How can I be a father to my children after being away for so long? What keeps me going more than anything else is the question: 'How can I reach everybody's hearts to end the existence of death row?'

They speak through me
Duma Kumalo

During 1984 there were demonstrations in Sharpville, not far from Johannesburg, against increased rents. I was involved in these demonstrations and when the police started shooting we decided we would take further action. We decided we would take the Councillor (who was being used by the Apartheid regime) down to the Councillor's home and demand action. When we got to his home, the police started shooting again and someone in the crowd was injured. I went to help this person and, while doing so, the Councillor was killed. Three months later I was charged with the murder of the Councillor. I was sentenced to death and remained on death row for three years. I was saved only fifteen hours prior to my execution.

Death row is like living in a graveyard. You are already dead. You are just waiting for someone to push you into the grave. 99% of the time I was prepared to die. It was my expectation and in some ways we died many times on death row. We were in pain every minute and I often thought that it would only be death that would provide an escape.

When we were told we were not going to be executed, it was unbelievable. It was hard to tell dreams from reality. Whenever we slept, we dreamt of being outside. But when we woke in the morning we were still on death row. So many things happened to us that we will never forget. You realise you are on the brink of death when they take your clothes from you and they give you the clothes of the dead. On one occasion they gave me two left shoes and when I pointed this out they said to me 'there is no walking here'.

At first I was filled with hatred but I was fortunate that I was surrounded by people who taught me about the politics of our country. These political understandings helped me make sense of my experience. We knew we were in a political struggle and we knew we were together in this. I learnt to identify that what was going on was much broader than my own life. Those in power had a collective hate towards us. And we, who had been condemned, could easily have developed and built upon a collective hate for our captors. But we saw that the hate of those in power made them do many stupid things and we realised that we did not want to hate like them. If we were as consumed with hate as they were, we realised that we might do very stupid things also!

As we struggled, we realised that it was those in power who would one day be condemned and this is how we survived. We reversed the power. We knew they expected us to hate, so when we learned to laugh about the painful things that had happened to us, it took away their influence over us.

When I am asked how this was possible, I think there were long histories of resistance for each of us. I would like to acknowledge my mother who was a maid somewhere in town. She would steal sugar, milk and bread for us and bring it home. On the weekends she would bring the white children's clothes home with her to wash and she would dress us in them. They would be our clothes over the weekend and only on Monday would they be returned to the city. During those days, if she had been caught, she would have been tried for treason. She took very high risks for her love of her children. Many of us on death row could remember the love of our parents and this helped us to survive those years.

It could not however save the lives of those who were executed. Day after day, others were taken to be hanged. We lost so many people. I was not aware at the time that one day I would be free. What drives me today is to tell the story. Maybe their soul is in me. Maybe when I open my mouth they do the talking. Maybe, through me, they can also be free.

Part Two: Reflections in the small groups

Here is a small sample of some of the comments and stories that were told in the small groups as a response to the stories told by Duma and Elias.

Truth-telling

I want to say thank you to those who shared their stories this morning. Your words put me in touch with my own efforts over years to stay in touch with hope in times of adversity. Sometimes in our country, Australia, we still face a lot of contradictions. Some of these relate to how to deal with structural racism and how to deal with the social conditions of our people. This makes many of us wonder how we can make a contribution to responding to these issues. I'm very proud to be here today and I am also very moved that my story is valued here. I want to say that the stories I heard today I will take back home with me to Australia. I will listen to your stories again in my own heart. I will say to myself: I met those men, I heard those stories, how can I learn from them? I have long admired the redemptive value of truth-telling. Telling my stories in a truthful and honest way has been really important to me. There are certain practices of truth-telling that contribute to healing, and for me they are also linked to spirituality. (Marlene, Australia)

Learning to 'live with'

Not long ago, I was on my own version of death row with AIDS and so I felt connected to this morning's stories. They made me think of the shame that many people in this country are living with because of HIV/AIDS. Because of the stigma surrounding HIV/AIDS many people keep their diagnosis secret and hidden. This brings me sorrow and also a sense of fear. I work as an AIDS counsellor and I have pride in those who are making it possible for people to live openly and positively with HIV. Dealing with AIDS is different than other political struggles. Those of us who are HIV positive must find ways of 'living with' AIDS rather than 'fighting against' it. I think we can all learn from each other. (Bongani, South Africa)

A Rwandan perspective

It was a considerable challenge to me to listen to the stories of the ex-prisoners. I am the only person of my immediate family to survive the Rwandan genocide. At first, I must say I wondered why on earth ex-prisoners had been asked to give the first talk at this conference. I was feeling quite tense about this. In Rwanda, we have 100,000 people imprisoned for the genocide that occurred in our country ten years ago. Many of us in Rwanda struggle to understand how those who committed the genocide could have caused such harm. As the ex-prisoners spoke this morning, I began to realise that I was very grateful that I could listen to their voices. I began to realise that I have never tried to think about the perspective of those who committed the crimes in Rwanda. In listening today, through overcoming some of my own prejudices, I have begun to feel more hopeful about my own country. (Jean-Baptiste, Rwanda)

Part Three: The song and reflections in the large group

A song was written in response to the stories of Elias and Duma, and this was sung at the beginning of Part Three. Its lyrics can be seen in the box on the following page.

The following reflections were then made in the large group:

- I liked the ways in which mothers' feisty resistance was acknowledged and honoured this morning. Often the resistance of women and mothers is not as visible as men's resistance. But it is powerfully significant and I so appreciated that this was spoken about this morning.

- I appreciated the ways in which people spoke about the significance of humour.

- I found frightening the images of nightmares and 'inner landscapes' that continued to haunt people after their release from prison. What are we doing to assist people to deal with these nightmares?

- The church has complicity in many stories of trauma in different parts of the world. I am interested in finding ways to address this.

- In Kwa Zulu Natal there are people serving 400 year sentences who are asking us to organise meetings with the people they hurt. They know they will probably never be released but these actions give their life meaning.

On the row of death

Living in a graveyard
Means you are already dead
Just waiting for someone
To push you into the grave

There are some things
We will never forget
I remember my two left shoes
I remember the feeling of no escape

We died many times
On the row of death
There we were condemned.
In our dreams we flew away
But then the morning came

Hope came through spirit or politics
Through being a collective
We found ways to turn it all around
Laughter is a beautiful sound

What drives me today
Is to tell the story
Maybe their soul is in me
When I open my mouth they do the talking
Through me they can be free

My mother was a maid somewhere in town
She'd steal food for us and bring it home
On the weekends the clothes she cleaned
Would become our own

We lost so many
We see them clearly
It is our duty to share their story

- It seems to me that our memories, even the most difficult, are sometimes what give us the drive to continue the journey of healing.

- As people have been speaking, I have found myself thinking of the people who spent years in the dungeons during the Apartheid era who would have been able to contribute to the development of our country. Now some of those people are sleeping in pipes and others say they are worth nothing. Those who say this do not understand.

Part Four: Final comments from Elias and Duma

Elias: The reflections that people have made, the stories they have told in response to my story, have been like a kind of treatment or medicine to me. As I listened, each story felt like a small dose to cure me from the events of my past.

Duma: Thank you for this opportunity as it is bringing back my dignity. I believe every story needs a listener and you have provided that to my story today. You have enabled me to speak truthfully about my life. Thank you.

The other themes

This sort of process then occurred around the following themes:

Exploring experiences of shame and guilt. In this session two people were interviewed in relation to the journey they have made and the steps they are taking in coming to terms with experiences of shame and guilt. Karin Penno-Burmeister from Germany spoke about her experience as the daughter of parents who were National Socialists and the work she now does at Ladelund Concentration Camp Memorial Centre honouring the victims of the Holocaust and linking descendants of those who were killed with descendents of the perpetrators. Christo Thesnarr spoke from the perspective of a white Afrikaans male and his work in coming to terms with the history and legacies of Apartheid.

Stories of transcendence. In this session two people were interviewed in relation to the journey they have taken in coming to terms with events in their past. Bounthanh Phommasathit spoke about her experiences of growing up in Laos during the time of the Indo-China war and her current work in Laos with a Vietnam Veteran, Lee Thorn, who was involved in the bombing of her village. And Marlene Jackamarra from Australia spoke of her experiences as an Indigenous Australian in coming to terms with the effects of the Stolen Generation – the forced separation of Aboriginal children from their families.

Stories of reconciliation. In this session two people were interviewed about the journey they have taken in relation to reconciliation. Andrew Rice spoke of his work with September 11 Families for Peaceful Tomorrows, while Pat McGee spoke of his involvement with the IRA and subsequent reconciliation work with the daughter of one of the men who was killed in an IRA bombing that Pat was involved in organising.

Reflections and songs were then woven around each of these themes so that by the end of the gathering a rich tapestry of stories had been created.

Looking beyond

Despite the diversity of stories told, it was acknowledged that there have been a number of struggles in recent times that have led to immense loss of life that were not discussed over the three days of this gathering. Throughout our days on Robben Island many of us were thinking of the current events in the Middle East and how future generations may be needing to hold gatherings to heal the memories of events occurring now due to war, occupation, trauma, political violence and torture.

While the gathering did not, and could not, explore the stories of all countries' memories of trauma, it did provide an opportunity for everyone present to witness the stories of others, to contribute reflections, and to participate in significant story-telling rituals which linked people's stories together in healing ways. One aspect of the conversations that resonated for many participants was the importance of remembering those who have died while attempting to bring about changes in their countries. This was a theme taken up by a Rwandan participant at the very end of the gathering and it was a sentiment that also shaped the lyrics of the 'journey of healing song'.

> *We would like to end this gathering by honouring all those loved ones who have died in the struggles of our countries. Can we pause for a minute to remember and revere all those who we have lost and who look over us?* Jean-Baptiste (Rwanda)

Journey of Healing Song

It's a journey that we're on

One that we don't take alone

So many have walked before us here

And future generations will carry on

This journey of healing

This song we are singing

We'll sing to this island

And to the sky

To the mountain

And the ocean

And to those who have long passed by

Last words

Picture if you can, a ferry making its way back from Robben Island to Cape Town. On board are 70 people from many different countries, all grateful for the opportunity to have shared the last three days together and all looking forward to reconnecting with loved ones and colleagues to continue the process of addressing histories of trauma in their own countries. For more information about the gathering and/or the work of the Institute for the Healing of Memories please consult their webpage: www.healingofmemories.co.za

Note

1. David's role on this gathering was to co-ordinate the documentation process. This involved the writing and recording of songs as well as the creation of a written document.

References

Denborough, D. 2002: 'Community song-writing and narrative practice.' *Clinical Psychology*, Issue 17, September.

Lapsley, M. 2002: 'The healing of memories.' *The International Journal of Narrative Therapy and Community Work*, No.2.

White, M. 2004: 'Working with people who are suffering the consequences of multiple trauma: A narrative perspective.' *The International Journal of Narrative Therapy and Community Work*, No.1.

Made in the USA
Las Vegas, NV
12 November 2020